Ex-formation

ars Müller Publishers

Kenya HARA

+

HARA Seminar in
The Department of
Science of Design
Musashino Art University

Foreword

Lars MÜLLER

It is a miracle that curiosity survives formal education.
——*Albert Einstein*

The education of designers has suffered for some time from an acute dearth of methodology, sufficing itself with imparting knowledge on the most rudimentary level. This failure to turn knowledge transfer into the spark igniting sublime imagination is what Kenya Hara sees as the reason for the current stagnation in communication creativity.

For the past ten years, Hara has been countering this kind of superficial learning and the random hunt for information fragments with a teaching concept marked by compelling lucidity and simplicity. Inquisitiveness takes the place of the indiscriminate assembling of facts, and a delight in sensual qualities takes priority over rational analysis. He calls this method "ex-formation," connoting a renunciation of the factual in favor of an ardent search after insights and ideas.

Free-flowing discussions and debates in the classroom on a range of surprising themes give rise in this way to unfettered and astonishing solutions and visualizations by the students. Many display a substantive incisiveness and aesthetic that bear the hallmark of the master himself. An intelligent brand of humor sometimes comes to the fore that betrays the students' casually confident approach to their assignments.

Kenya Hara makes curiosity–the will to perceive and understand as a basic human resource–the driving force for the students' confrontation with themselves, their own power of imagination, and the conditions for creatively implementing their visions. The result is solutions that do not cater to the viewers' stock of shared information but which instead challenge them to continually discover something new.

As a designer and teacher myself, I regard Kenya Hara's model as an exemplary template for instilling in students in all design disciplines, from communication and product design to architecture, an independent and creative design attitude.

And as a publisher, I feel obliged to devote myself to the methodological and theoretical principles of design education.

Ex-formation
Communication Method by Making Things Unknown

Kenya H A R A

Designer
Professor at Musashino Art University

What moves people's hearts, in every case, is the unknown.

Things that people already know don't excite them. And yet people have great zeal for making the world known. These days, with the continual growth and development of media, every event, every matter, every phenomenon, is turned into information and disseminated at high speed and high density. Through continual contact with these pieces of information, people constantly replace the unknown world with known matters or phenomena. To know something is to cause to our sensory perceptions the fertilization of an inspirational, pounding emotion. However, whether it's because the provision of information has surpassed critical mass, without us realizing it, knowledge has ceased functioning as an intermediary that facilitates thought, and multitudes of those pieces of information pile up all around us, their state one in which it's not clear whether they are dead or alive.

If so, wouldn't it be a good thing to *unknow* the world? I tried putting forth that query in a university setting. In a seminar format course at Musashino Art University's Department of the Science of Design, I had the students, who were in their final year, consider the concept of unknowing the world as a communication design question. Naturally, because it was an experiment, we couldn't know definitely whether it would succeed or fail, but the project itself was expected, as a fresh question, to begin to move us, helping us ask about the meanings of knowing and understanding, and the essence of information.

The End of Thought

Modern people love to say, "I know, I know." Why? Because you can say "I know" two times in a row. About the architect Le Corbusier? "I know, I know." And about the paella eaten at a coastal food court in Barcelona, massages in resort hotels in Chiang Mai, the sparkly hologram seal on monetary bills…. Every time you begin to speak about anything, you feel assailed by the feeling you're going to be told, "I know, I know." Are people today that full of knowledge? The truth is, we spend our days receiving innumerable pieces of information. Thanks to the proliferation of media and the exuberance of news coverage, each and every activity around the world flies about, all of them like bits of grass spat out of a lawnmower, ending up as scattered data fragments in the media space. Whether our minds like it or not, they are unavoidably, incessantly touched by these data fragments. As a result, the high frequency of our contact with data is related to the adherence to our minds of vast multitudes of scraps of information to our minds. As an index of knowledge, if they function to arouse further interest, we might be able to proactively assess the value of accumulating these data fragments. However, if we observe a little calmly, if we only engage with the fact that we are touched by information, the conversation won't be able to move forward from there. "I know, I know" shuts down the conversation, acting entirely like a full stop to thought.

Acquiring Knowledge is not the Goal

"I heard Zaha Hadid is working on the new Tokyo Olympic stadium." "I know, I know. The Beijing Olympic stadium was done by Herzog right?" "Herzog and de Meuron. They're a Swiss architecture group, huh? They're the ones who did the Aoyama Plaza too." "I know, I know." "The Soho Plaza in New York is by Koolhaas." "I know, I know." "By the way it seems that next month the Tokyo National Museum in Ueno will exhibit the folding screens, Pine Trees." "I know. Tohaku Hasegawa's best known work, right?" "I've really been getting into *india* ink painting. The other day, I saw Okyo's work in Kyoto, too." "I know, I know. Maruyama Okyo's monkey paintings are great, aren't they?" "I think his peacock paintings are more famous, like *Peacocks and Peonies*." "Amazing! I so respect you! Yamamoto, you're also really knowledgeable about traditional sweets—" "Oh, you're talking about the Pierre Hermé ISPAHAN—that was really delicious, right?" "I know, I know. It was in a magazine, and I bragged to my friends that I'd tried it!"

As a conversation, this sounds fun, and there was plenty of variety and knowledge, but maybe because the utterance "I know, I know" exhibits a sense of accomplishment, it functions to prompt the interlocutor to present other knowledge or end the conversation and call for diversion to another issue. The person who offers the topic, too, is only introducing facts. So the conversation is simply the mutual putting forth of known information, with no intersection. The proffered information is a little extreme, but we've all had plenty of experience with these kinds of conversations.

Intrinsically, knowledge is merely the entrance to thought. A conversation is that which helps interlocutors exercise one another's thinking by exchanging words, initiated by trivial, commonplace knowledge; by kneading together knowledge that is no more than fragments through dialogue or speculation, we will be able to reach out to our imagination in the realm of the unknown. That is, "to know things" is where the imagination starts, not the goal. Even so, just as is symbolized by these conversations filled with, "I know, I know," we somehow ended up derailed from the route that helps direct knowledge to be sublimated to imagination, and are stopping the train of thought. The person putting forth is zealous only about tossing fragmented pieces of information to the other, and the person receiving makes it one of his or her goals to catch them. Before we realize it, we've stopped the continual and difficult kneading and begun a consistent game of *information catch*. Perhaps this is where the stagnation in communication creativity is lurking.

Creating an Entrance for Curiosity

Here's one more thing. This time, rather than conversations, I will imagine familiar examples of information design. For instance, the guidebook including the information necessary for a trip. Let's call it, *An Easy Strolling Guide to New York; Become a New Yorker with just one volume.* As a guidebook for experienced travelers who want to travel and stroll on their own, it contains an enormous amount of rationally edited and easily retrievable information.

It begins with the introduction of LaGuardia Airport and John F. Kennedy International Airport and ways to access the city. Specifically, it describes the uses and fares of taxis, buses, and subways. Following the introduction of indicative exchange rates, temperature graphs, and standard tipping is hotel information. Hotels are classified by the number of stars, ranging from super high-quality hotels to cheap ones, and in some cases, youth hostels. A remarkably large volume of the writing offers information about food, extending from famous seafood or steak restaurants to recommended spots in Chinatown and Little Italy; places to enjoy the cuisines of Scandinavia, Japan, India, Mexico, and France; fast-food joints; popular delis and bagel shops; and even take-out soup places, with the collected details extending to these establishments' interiors and pricing. Shopping information is organized by areas and streets. It goes without saying that the map has been designed and edited so it's easy to read. Information about cultural facilities, including art museums, is smartly organized, covering everything from musical and concert programs to nightspots and even recommended spas. The inclusion of reports of SoHo's latest circumstances or the vigor of Midtown's open-air markets responds to the expectations of readers eager for current information. Then there is pullout information: reader-suggested urban strolling routes and Central Park jogging courses.

It was self-described information architect Richard Saul Wurman who said, "The goal of information design is to empower the user." Naturally, I basically agree with his view, and am sure that an efficiently compiled guidebook would serve New York sightseers as a valuable navigation tool. Guidebook in hand, they would experience New York: visiting alternative spaces in Midtown, eating a bucket of mussels at South Street Seaport, picking up a few things at a museum shop, and roaming around SoHo. Home again, before long, with these experiences as their resources, they would bounce through question-centered conversations: "Did you buy spices at an open-air market?" "Did you stay at the Standard High Line Hotel? Did you go to the Mercer Street Salon?" "Did you see the Gansevoort Market Meat Center?" "Did you go to the new MUJI?"

Probably you too can imagine how happily their conversation swings along through its unlimited supply of *I knows*. They toss questions to one another, each to be answered by "I know, I know." Behind their conversation is a perceptible satisfaction in the understanding that they have successfully replaced the pretravel guidebook lessons with actual experience. It goes without saying that this kind of conversation has to be enjoyable in a way. To these people, traveling is sightseeing, period. Their desire is to see expected scenes. We cannot say that a serious documentary approach is of higher quality than the approach of these people in just looking for what they expect.

However, would it be possible, by bluntly disregarding the cycle of exchanging already-known information, the "I-know" cycle, to create a guidebook that would act as an entrance for curiosity, one that would help readers sense a fresher, unknown New York? I suppose it would be something that in the end does not make New York known, but rather awakens us quietly, yet thoroughly, to the truth of how little we know about the metropolis of New York.

How to *Unknow* the World

Is communication possible which, rather than making the world known, makes people understand how little they know of the world? This book is an attempt to answer that question. If you can figure out how much you don't know, the method by which you will know it will appear naturally. As Socrates said, the only true wisdom is in knowing that you know nothing. And there is power in this sort of ignorance. There are countless ways to finally reach knowledge; how one arrives there in the end is up to each individual. This concept calls for a complete turnaround on conventional communication methods. I named this method *Ex-formation* to act as a counterpart to *Information*. *Ex* vs. *In*. *Exform* vs. *Inform*. That is, I'd like to think of the form and function of information not in terms of making known, but in terms of making unknown.

The Department of The Science of Design and the Hara Seminar

I'd like to turn to the content of the Hara Seminar, advancing this discussion as a single research documentary revolving around Ex-formation. Since 2003, in addition to my own design work, I've begun to spend time with students at my alma mater. Here, I'm not teaching, but rather taking the opportunity to think about subjects that I can only think about in this context, inviting the younger generation to join me. I conduct a seminar with those fourth-year students who want to share a theme of my choosing. Of course, it's not bad to have the students choose their own themes for their graduation projects, and have the teacher follow, because it means we may come across unpredictable themes. However, as a university is a research organization, I thought that it would be just as well for the teacher to further exercise his or her independence as a researcher. A teacher shares with his or her students a long-studied theme that he or she takes seriously. The work will be as tough as the teacher is serious, and it might really be a challenge for the students. That is why the theme of the 2004 Hara Seminar was narrowed down to *Ex-formation*. Its definition was as yet undetermined and its concept obscure. How to treat a theme never approached before would depend on how the teacher and students collaborated. I gathered fourteen students who understood this premise.

We are in the Science of Design department. Generally, design departments' names are prefaced with genre-specific words, like *graphic, product, image,* or *textile,* but our department is not, because design is a single, indivisible concept. This concept states that design is to explore the possibilities of new modes of perception, as well as methods of expression in all fields that involve the disciplines of environmental design and communication, and that design practices encompassing many different fields are interwoven, connected at the root. Our curriculum is organized to realize this philosophy; it's based on an inquiry into the ideal intellectual background for professionals expected to participate in environmental formation or communication.

The content of our curriculum stands out among art educational institutions. Design theory is at its center, and interspersed are required subjects whose connection with the general sciences is recognized, including theories of phase and autopoiesis and the thought methods of meta-languages such as semiotics and discourse representation theory. Two types of practicum surround design theory: visual design as relevant to communication, and product design as relevant to industry. Students choose curriculums that match their interests. This is also a process in which they discover, on their own, the design profession they wish to pursue.

The content of the current curriculum was developed and brought forth through academic process in our institution by Shutaro Mukai, who studied design at the Ulm School of Design in Germany. Now, those of us who graduated from the Science of Design under Shutaro

Mukai play the role of both inheriting and developing his ideas. The domain of that role has been vastly expanded, transcending the idea of simply nurturing designers as the bearers of design techniques. Our graduates participate in a variety of activities that come to be under the context of design, not only as designers but also as planners, researchers, curators, scholars, editors and producers; our role here on campus is to cultivate and nurture people who will challenge the world through *design* as a branch of wisdom.

The last elective in the curriculum, for students in their final year, is a seminar course presided over by a full-time teacher. This course acts as the students' final graduation project. My specialties are design theory and communication design, but, through the themes we deal with in this course, I approach the actual issues of current information design.

Ten Themes

We've conducted Ex-formation research continuously between 2003 and 2014. Over the years, we've tackled various themes. Themes are determined through a circular process of dialogue and voting. On the

wall, we tape up scraps of paper noting words the teacher and students are
interested in exploring. Via the dialogue/voting process, somewhat like
the boiling and then simmering of a soup, we distill our annual theme.
Each year, fourteen or fifteen students have come to participate in this
attempt to *make things unknown*, taking individual approaches to the
theme of the year.

Below are the themes of the past decade.

1 : RIVER (Shimanto River)
2 : RESORT
3 : WRINKLES
4 : PLANTS
5 : NUDITY
6 : WOMAN
7 : HALF-DONE
8 : AIR
9 : PAIR
10 : TOKYO

When we say that *the scales fall from the eyes*, we mean that we are freed from our preconceptions and are able to feel anew the reality of this world. My students, challenging themselves with these themes, competed to achieve this freedom. I cannot present the work of all of the students here, but would like to retrace the research in digest fashion.

RIVER (Shimanto River)

For Ex-formation, any theme will do, as long as it involves information of which we have a preconceived notion, something we know, or are accustomed to, something we assume is *this sort of thing, probably.* The theme could be car, Greece, water, or honeymoon. The goal is to make it unknown. The first year's motif was *river,* or more specifically, the famous Shimanto River. Why? The genesis was *Japan's Last Pristine River,* a memorable T V documentary my students and I watched together. But none of us had ever been there. That was enough of a motive for us. We can assume that British people living in London who have never been to Scotland's Loch Ness still have some image of it in mind. The Shimanto River is to us as Loch Ness is to most Londoners. How do we unknown a preexisting image?

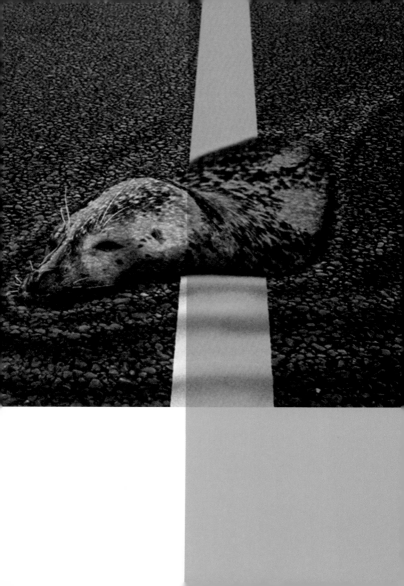

1 Simulations: If the River Were a Road

Shinsaku INABA
Sousuke MATSUSHITA
Hirofumi MORI

The memory of familiar things functions as a yardstick that helps us infer the dimensions and forms of all things. Our memory of asphalt roads, for example, functions this way. From our driving experiences, certain things have permeated our brains as memories: the coarseness of the road and the width, length, and intervals between the white lines. Thus, the white lines on the road act as the measure of perception that lets us know the speed or distance between cars by way of the velocity and pitch of these lines as they move in our field of vision. This team noticed this fact. The river inlaid with an asphalt road conveys the river's size and shape much more vividly than would ordinary photographs. We get an image of the undulation of the meandering river with a sense of realism, as if we were taking the wheel, and the dozens of lanes filling the width of the river near its mouth look like an airport runway. As a result, rather than understanding, we have the reality of the terrain dramatically etched in our minds, like a scar formed upon the brain.

The white lines on the road's surface
function as a measuring stick that
helps us understand the size of a thing.
Above is the source of the river.
The white line indicates its scale.

RIVER | Simulations: If the River Were a Road

RIVER | Simulations: If the River Were a Road

Without even thinking, we see the river,
feeling sort of like we're driving a car.
Our normal way of looking at the river is reformed.

RIVER | Simulations: If the River Were a Road

The dam looks like a parking
lot, the wide mouth of the
river like an airport.
On the left are actual photos.

2　Footprint Landscape: Stepping on the Shimanto River

Kyoko NAKAMURA
Kazuko NOMOTO
Kaori HASHIMOTO

This team made footprint mask blocks, each black acrylic plate sporting a hole the size of an actual footprint. Members then placed and photographed these plates on various locations along the Shimanto River basin. By reorganizing these photos of a tremendous number of ground surfaces collected by footprint, the students reproduced the feeling of the shore. The footprint-shaped cutouts of the ground visually evoke the tactile sensation of walking barefoot. By framing a fish in one of the footprints, the students created a significant awareness of it as something to be trod upon. Because the photograph is not of the whole area but rather indicates both the object and the route of perception, viewers reflexively simulate that action in their minds.

The fish shown as an object to be trod upon awakens our perceptions in various ways, including the sense of touch. If it were placed on a plate instead, it would probably arouse other types of perceptions. This team is unique in its viewpoint, by which it intended to present the river as an object to be trod upon.

At one time, by walking barefoot, humankind picked up information from the surface of the Earth through the soles of the feet.

RIVER | Footprint Landscape: Stepping on the Shimanto River

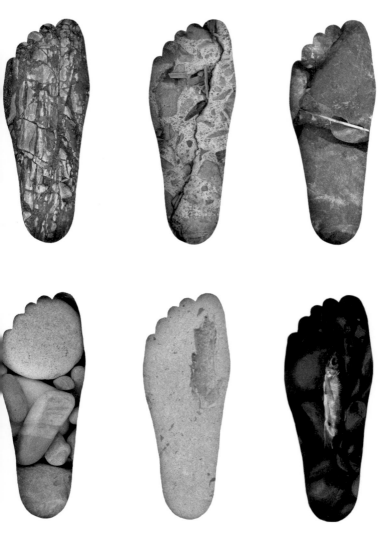

RIVER | Footprint Landscape: Stepping on the Shimanto River

Stepping on plants

RIVER | Footprint Landscape: Stepping on the Shimanto River

Do you want to step on it?
Does it feel good?
Does it hurt?

RIVER | Footprint Landscape: Stepping on the Shimanto River

3   Collecting

Akari OHNO
Asako TADANO

Waste, or rather fragments of man-made materials, are widely scattered around the globe. We cannot escape their range, whether on the peak of Chomolungma or the bottom of the Mariana Trench. So it's not a question of whether or not there is trash; we can effectively know a place by asking, "What kind of garbage is it and what are its circumstances?" This team has presented the Shimanto River by diligently collecting man-made objects discarded along its basin and coolly analyzing them, like a crime scene investigation squad. Specifically, team members collected samples, using the areas surrounding the river's twenty-one bridges as bases. They photographically recorded the context in which things were lying about, then collected the actual objects. Through the dispassionate classification of objects by type, period since disposal, degree of change due to corrosion and wear and conditions resulting from contact with natural objects, including stones and sand, and further reorganization along an abstract, straightened representation of the river, they bring an unknown river into sight. By peering at this garbage, we gain an understanding of the Shimanto River environs, compared to those of our own local rivers.

Takahi-chinkabashi
Kumaaki-chinkabashi
Nagano-chinkabashi
Ittohyo-chinkabashi
Ichubara-chinkabashi
Wakai-chinkabashi
Hirose-chinkabashi
Jyogu-chinkabashi
Mukaiyama-chinkabashi
Satokawa-chinkabashi
Kayabukute-chinkabashi
Mishima-chinkabashi
Hage-chinkabashi
Nakahage-chinkabashi
Nagaoi-chinkabashi
Iwama-chinkabashi
Kuchiyanai-chinkabashi
Katsuma-chinkabashi
Takase-chinkabashi
Misato-chinkabashi
Sada-chinkabashi

Distance from river mouth /
bridge length

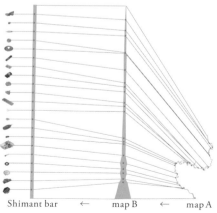

Shimant bar   ←   map B   ←   map A

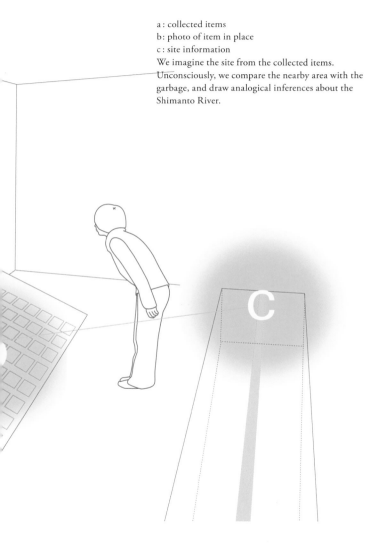

a : collected items
b : photo of item in place
c : site information
We imagine the site from the collected items.
Unconsciously, we compare the nearby area with the garbage, and draw analogical inferences about the Shimanto River.

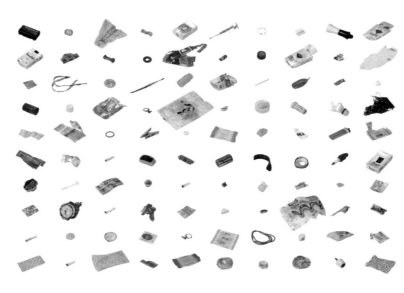

Ten items of trash picked up around each of
the twenty-one chinkabashi (low water crossings) are
arranged in lines in the same order as the bridges.
Through this array of 210 pieces of garbage,
the team reproduces the Shimanto River.

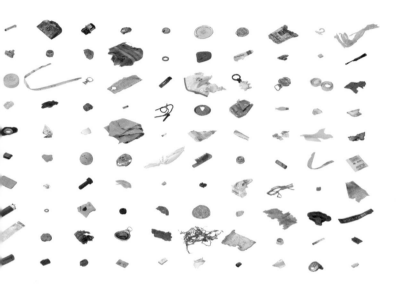

4   Hexahedron:
The Shimanto River Cut into Cubes

Aiko YOSHIHARA

Making the twenty-one bridges her bases, Aiko Yoshihara took photos at fixed points and turned the Shimanto River into data by reconfiguring the photos into regular hexahedrons, or cubes. She placed the camera on three points of each bridge (both sides and center) and photographed the scenery in six directions (forward [downriver], backward, right, left, up and down). These photos were affixed to the six facets of a cube. The idea is to let us experience the river through handling the cubes; we can arrange them as a reproduction of the scenery from the bridges where they were created, in twenty-one rows of three cubes each, or play with them like building blocks, placing them in random groups. When expressed as a lineup from upper to lower reaches, the blocks have a moderate mixture of the consistency of images and the abstract quality of scenery reorganized into a cube; thus, the vision we form of the river from these objects is mysterious, semi-abstract and semi-concrete. However, once we understand the rules of the photography, we can maintain a perspective on the river that gives us a consciousness of both consistency and inconsistency that differs from conventional photographic expression.

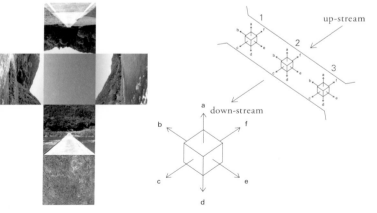

RIVER | Hexahedron: The Shimanto River Cut into Cubes

One can draw analytical
inferences about the
Shimanto River's environment
through three views of the sky:
from the beginning of the bridge,
to the far end of it.

RIVER | Hexahedron: The Shimanto River Cut into Cubes

By knocking over and re-stacking the cubes,
like building blocks, one develops an optical illusion,
as if deconstructing the landscape
of the Shimanto River.
Through the actual manipulation of the landscape,
a new understanding of the Shimanto River is born.

RIVER | Hexahedron: The Shimanto River Cut into Cubes

5   Catch and Eat 6
Six Days Alone : The Document

Kouichirou UNO

Kouichirou Uno erected a tent in one location and stayed there for six days. He planned to obtain his sustenance (except drinking water) by fishing the river. It was his first contact with this river, and he had no prior experience with either camping by a river or fishing in one. It seemed a bit far-fetched that he was going to catch fish with nothing but a fishing kit he bought in Tokyo for about ¥1,000 (US $8 / €6). Thanks to the cooperation of locals living near his tent site, he learned—and put into practice—both fishing methods and the fundamentals of associating with the river.

Surpassing his expectations, Uno was able to increase his daily catch, and he was able to secure all of his food from the river. In his documentary record, he expresses the number and type of fish caught as a graph. The report includes objective facts such as the recipes he used to cook them and the change in his own weight. He narrates his daily experiences as a monologue. Uno is, so to speak, an utter stranger to the Shimanto River and thus represents us, the audience. Reading through his account, we recognize the atmosphere and feel as if it is we who have begun a life on the banks of the Shimanto River.

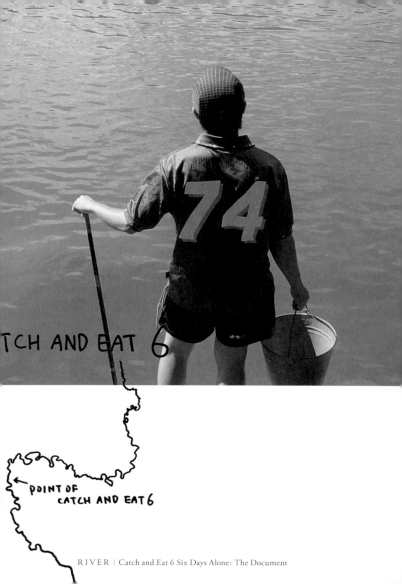

TCH AND EAT 6

POINT OF
CATCH AND EAT 6

Looking for a fishing spot…

It takes quite a while
to grill fish.

Using the bucket
as a pot

A stray cat
is after the fish.

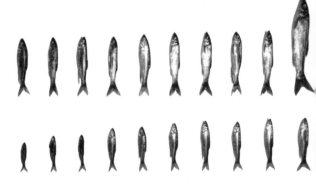

The catch: 28 fish

It's a sentimental journey.

RIVER | Catch and Eat 6 Six Days Alone: The Document

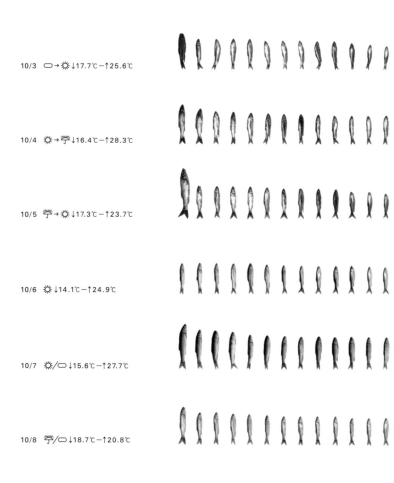

10/3　◯→☼↓17.7℃−↑25.6℃

10/4　☼→☂↓16.4℃−↑28.3℃

10/5　☂→☼↓17.3℃−↑23.7℃

10/6　☼↓14.1℃−↑24.9℃

10/7　☼/◯↓15.6℃−↑27.7℃

10/8　☂/◯↓18.7℃−↑20.8℃

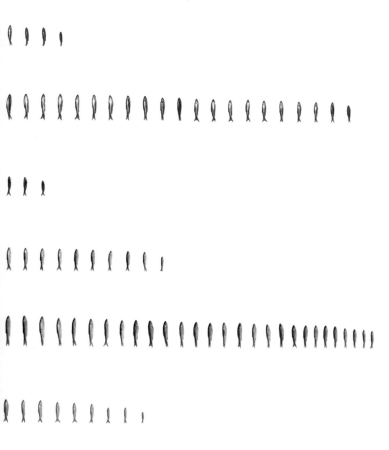

Personal story: I spent six days during which, aside from condiments,
I only ate things that came from the river. I drank vegetable juice, energy
drinks, and carbonated beverages that I bought from a vending machine.
I didn't become unhealthy, but I did lose three kilograms in six days.

RIVER | Catch and Eat 6 Six Days Alone: The Document

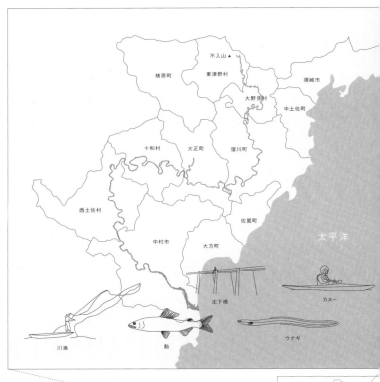

Standard Information about the Shimanto River
Here, in order to completely clarify the difference
between information and Ex-formation,
we present standard information about our theme.
The Shimanto River, in Kochi Prefecture
in Japan's Shikoku region, is 186 kilometers long.
It is known as Japan's last pristine river,
and is straddled by twenty-one so-called "sinking bridges,"
designed without guard rails to allow water to flow over them
in times of flooding.

RIVER | Catch and Eat 6 Six Days Alone: The Document

RESORT

The theme for the second year of Ex-formation was resort.

Some stereotypical images might be: paradise, comfortable, loose, extraordinary, exoticism, schedule-free, a sense of loose fit, dissolved in harmony, in touch with Mother Nature, clear and transparent, serene, divine and venerable, wasteful, lazy, fully matured, luxuriant flora, rustling trees, the soles of the feet, the tips of the fingers, taste on the tongue, textures, moist, velvety, slimy, smooth and dry, sweet scents....

Instead of these, my students presented those small everyday moments when we release a small sigh of relief in our souls. People do experience those moments of repose without flying all the way to some tropical seaside thick with palm trees or finding a comfortable lounge on which to stretch out poolside. It seemed to me that we should call those moments *seeds of resort*, as it is these instances that make people feel deeply relaxed and serene from the very center of their beings. Thus began the study of *resort* as a place in which one is able to sense the ocean in a narrow bed or paradise in a single glass of water.

1 Vinyl / Stripes

Emiko AI

Looking at the line of photos, we all felt a deep surge of empathy. At a glance, we understand that the hues and textures of colorful vinyl possess a strange charm, creating a liberating feeling that emancipates the senses. Featured in the photos are a variety of colored sandals, brilliant plastic cups, a blue and white parasol, brightly striped tropical fish, and so on. The persuasive power of the visual surpasses the eloquence of logic.

Ai's research went on to simulate images to project the colors or textures of vinyl and stripes onto actual scenes of daily life. The series, entitled "Turning Tokyo into Vinyl and Stripes," included such unique objects as a road sign and a shop sign, all of whose textures and colors were transformed into vinyl and stripes. I laughed in spite of myself, and emerging in this laugh was an essence of *resort* never noticed before.

Familiar things are vinyled and striped.
The photo is of a road sign.

When the road map is inflated with vinyl material,
it looks cheerful for some reason.

安全 ✚ 第一

2 Sleeping Outside

Makiko ORIHARA
Yukari KIMURA
Satoko TAKAHASHI
Hiroko MORI

This team's research topic was sleeping in the daytime, and outdoors, an activity that gives us a different kind of pleasure than we get from nighttime sleeping.

The team started its research by observing people lying on the grass in a park. The number of people peaked when the weather was best, and fell in concert with the sunlight and the temperature. Few outdoor sleepers were alone. The charms of sleeping outside are those that enhance sleeping itself, like companions, the right amount of sunshine and breeze, and a beautiful green landscape.

Once aware of these facts, the team collaborated in creating a dedicated outdoor sleeping tool it named *nap*. Carrying their naps, team members went out to nap in fields and meadows, on the decks of ships, urban rooftops, and university campuses. Every nap is chronicled in photographs and text. An interesting point they made in their report is that people share the pleasure of sleeping outside within the solidarity of sleeping with others. It may be that both humans and elephant seals share in the pleasure of sleeping in herds in the bright sunshine.

21.9℃ 22.9℃ 22.7℃

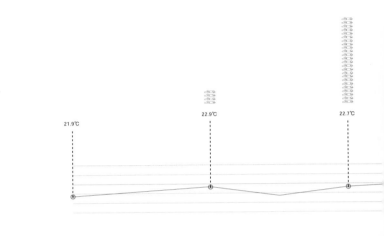

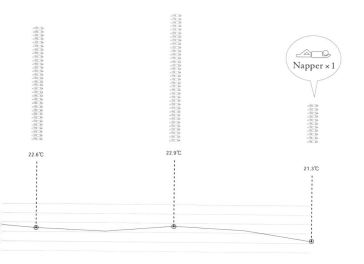

Napper × 1

22.6℃   22.9℃   21.3℃

RESORT | Sleeping Outside

On a city rooftop,
napping while listening to the car
horns bleating on the streets.

On the deck of a ship plying
Tokyo Bay,
napping to the sound of the engine
and the sight of fluttering flags.

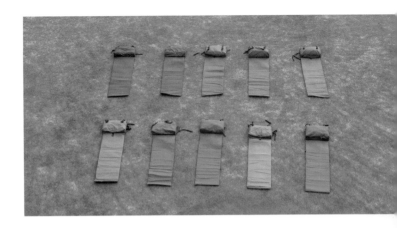

Sleeping with others outside is a different thing than the sleep we get alone at night. Even if everyone has his or her own style, there's a peace of mind we get from the presence of someone at our side.

RESORT | Sleeping Outside

3   Soft Creamer

Shino ITO
Aya KAZAMA
Mona TANAKA

Soft-serve ice cream *is* resort. This team began its research with this simple statement of intuition. Truly, there are very few things that so dexterously pull people from the ordinary world to the doorstep of pleasure. Previously in the seminar, we had touched on the theme of sunglasses. The moment we put on sunglasses, the world is defamiliarized. Soft-serve ice cream has the same effect. The photo of the salaried worker in an office corridor holding a soft-serve cone precisely reflects how it feels when resort is inserted into the ordinary.

This team's research pursued the question of how to design the semisolid cream. By focusing on the form of the nozzle through which the cream is extruded, and the motion of the hand by which the cream is received, team members came up with some innovative designs. The ultimate solution was one in which the shape of the cone on the bottom exactly replicates that of the cream on top. It's a design of superb metaphor, leading one from the ordinary to an ephemeral resort.

Everybody looks happy
with a soft-serve cone!

This is the kind of soft-serve ice cream you get when the nozzle is circular and you move your hand in a figure eight.

   A ribbon-shaped soft-serve cone is created when the nozzle is corrugated on one side and the receiving hand makes a simple alternating motion.

RESORT | Soft Creamer

This is what happens when
the nozzle has multiple small holes
and the receiving hand moves randomly.

This nozzle has a grooved cylinder.
When the receiving hand moves
in a spiral, elaborate details are created.

RESORT | Soft Creamer

Here's an image of multiple spirals of soft-serve ice cream. You get the feeling that the ice cream will fit perfectly into a cone designed as a spiral.

What you see is what you get:
This was designed to give the impression
that the soft-serve ice cream is packed
into the cone, right to the bottom.

RESORT | Soft Creamer

In Japan, there's a popular food called takoyaki, after which these cones are modeled. They're for bite-sized soft-serve ice cream.

By likening this tiny cone to takoyaki,
surely recognition of it as a one-bite
snack will spread smoothly,
breeding familiarity.

RESORT | Soft Creamer

RESORT | Soft Creamer

4   Resort Switch

Makoto TOMITA

Starting with the idea of adding a resort mode to various instruments, Makoto Tomita examined the relationship between human beings and machines. From imagining the resort switch on various devices, he tried to discover clues to the interaction of humans and instruments. Tomita's idea originated in the yuragi (fluctuating breeze) mode of an electric fan, which makes the motions and speed of a fan irregular and unpredictable. Changeable like nature's breeze, this is comfortable for us. As we come to value irregularity, we find resort lurking between humans and machines. On a TV, the resort switch makes the images gradually and imperceptibly fade into white; eventually the screen goes dark, giving us a wavering moment of gentle, sleep-inducing light and lessening the lonely silence that normally falls so suddenly when a TV is switched off. This is design located between ON and OFF. On the telephone the resort switch activates harmonious background music, so if your interlocutor is a close friend or relative, the music makes for a nice mood. This idea of a resort button may just be hypothetical speculation, but it does offer a new design method.

The yellow button says RESORT.
It puts the fan in yuragi mode.
Relaxed regularity leads to
a therapeutic interaction.

RESORT | Resort Switch

The RESORT switch adds
Hawaiian background music,
inviting relaxed conversation.

It's lonely for single people when the TV is abruptly shut off.
The RESORT switch gradually turns off the monitor,
first gradually filling the screen with white light.

RESORT | Resort Switch

What happens when you press the button?
The creator sets up the buttons first, and then considers their functions. Finally he thinks about the relationship between humans and equipment.

From this project, I imagine that maybe
artificial intelligence is more affectionate towards
people than people are.

RESORT | Resort Switch

WRINKLES

Life is full of tension. Plants grow and spread their lush green leaves, bloom brightly, and in time splendidly bear fruit. The culture and civilization through which human beings celebrate life is also represented a an aspiration for tension. We like brand-new clothes, young girls, newly finished buildings, freshly hand-made pure white paper, brand-new shoes.... These images are sources of what is bright, beautiful, and desirable. We want to live forever, surrounded by things like this. And so i has always been for mankind. And yet the rhythm of the cosmos coldly moves forward, always forward. Clothes become soiled, people age, buildings decay, even brand-new shoes are sullied in the hustle and bustle of the street. Without exception, *tension* becomes *wrinkle*.

Humans face this impermanence, meditating on their raw and fateful sorrow.

However, from this transient process the world can be read afresh, once we find and accept the rhythm of transference and resurrection, generation and degeneration.

1   Egg : A Collection of Wrinkles

Yukimi KUSHIGE

This is a collection of wrinkles. It is unique in its perfect choice of background—eggs—for the figures—wrinkles. Eggs are a symbol of tension. They are not spherical. An egg is spherical only in that its structure, with its thin hard external frame, has a certain strength. However, its spindle shape, not a perfectly spherical form, allows it to pass easily, and has a certain imbalance so that it won't roll away when it drops out. Eggs have the tranquil bearing of divinity and should be adored as objects within which life is nurtured. Because it would be fatal to the creature inside if even the tiniest wrinkle or deformation were to appear on this spindle shape, any and all living creatures, seeing such a malformation, would turn to stare in alarm, unable to look away, focused only on that defect. Herein lies the appeal of this study. Wrinkles are presented as the antithesis of tension. Yukimi Kushige's artistry at collecting wrinkles on the surface of egg (wrinkles shaped like Chinese cabbage, ears, and crevices) takes our breath away.

An egg is a symbol of tension of which
everyone has a sensuous memory.

With just a single wrinkle,
the tension of the egg's surface is
definitely lost.
Small thing, big impact.

Dents and depressions are in the same
category as wrinkles.
Even the gently indented egg,
no matter how tiny its dent is, is uncanny.

See the opening of
deeply wrinkled leaves
as cabbages grow.
Wrinkles make us feel life.

The wrinkles of the ear are not
random or disorganized, but
ordered and functional.

This wrinkle forms cleavage.
Its surface slopes gently,
but the structure is hidden deep inside.

The slightly altered egg makes us shudder.
The wrinkle overflows with vitality.
Eggs with these wrinkles
are packaged en masse here.

2 Wrinkled Products

Koutarou FUJITA
Kazuya MORITA
Yojiro WATANABE

This team created fresh surprises by calmly observing wrinkles, whic
carry a negative connotation, and inserting them into designs for ever
day articles.

The washboard is superb; its convex-concave undulations, on which cloth
would be scrubbed, have the appearance of wrinkled cloth. These wrinkle
referencing the folds of the Buddha's canonical robes, are truly beautifu
The compact has a mysterious presence, with wrinkles leading into
hole-like indentation, making us sense the existence of a creature. It tic
les the imagination when we think of touching it with a soft brush. Th
wrinkles on the popsicle are vivid physical reminders of the process
melting and freezing, recrystallizing the contents into the shape of th
packaging. These designs stimulate an odd part of our memory and e
periences, recalling for us cement that's dried inside its pouch, or wat
that's been frozen in a plastic bag. The idea of transferring the wrinkl
of the palm pressed to a glass onto the surface of an iron is interesting
well. It's a unique idea, to focus on wrinkles as a metaphor for *pressure*.

This is an example of wrinkles on a washboard
carved to look like Buddha's robes.
Its form is also beautiful,
like a statue of Buddha.

These are washboard designs.
The washboard cannot be wrinkled like cloth, but I adm
her perception of what it represents. A laugh escapes spo
taneously, because it awakens memories of days past.

WRINKLES | Wrinkled Products

This wrinkle looks kind of like a living thing.
Touching it with a brush gives a strange,
ticklish feeling.

A popsicle has melted and frozen again, giving the package a second shape by tracing its wrinkles. It would be interesting to mass-produce this.

In this case, the wrinkles of the palm of the hand have been applied to an iron's soleplate. Memory and observation. Then application.

3 Complex Trails: The Rivers and Roads of Japan

Chie UCHIDA

Aki TAKADA

Approximately three-quarters of Japan's land is mountainous. The falling rains flow through the lowlands and eventually into the sea. This plenitude of mountains leads to the etching of rivers into the land, like innumerable wrinkles. Japan's elaborate shape materializes when these rivers are traced.

On the other hand, the Japanese archipelago is home to more than 120 million people, living and doing. They wriggle on the surface of the ground, developing farmland, building and connecting rural roads, constructing cities, and circulating among them on highways. Human beings, with their activities and repetitive movements, have chiseled another kind of wrinkle into the land: roads, the wrinkles of the populace. These earth wrinkles originated differently than those nature has wrought. This team's research involved extracting these two types of wrinkles from a 1:200,000 map. The result is a clear and accurate illustration of the shape of the Japanese archipelago made up of two layers of wrinkles. Some excerpted areas are exhibited side by side. Because there is no unnecessary commentary, we naturally begin to imagine the backstories of these two kinds of wrinkles.

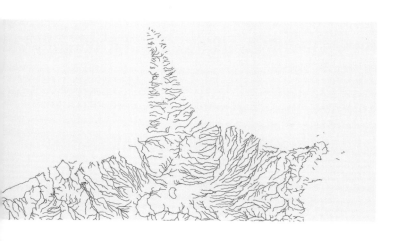

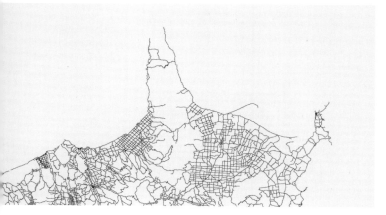

Above: river wrinkles
Below: road wrinkles
Rivers stretch vertically from the mountains to the sea.
Man-made roads sometimes form grids, and they follow the coastline.

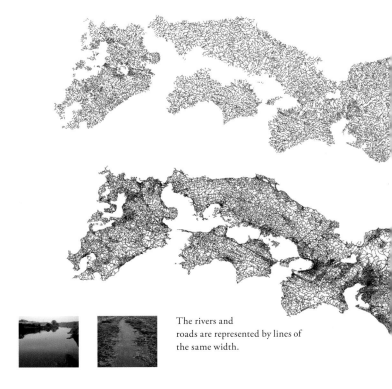

The rivers and
roads are represented by lines of
the same width.

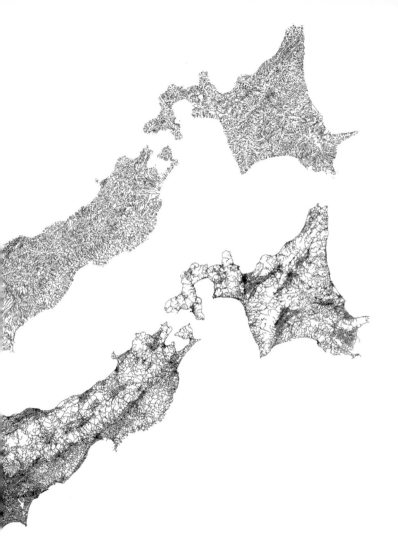

WRINKLES | Complex Trails : The Rivers and Roads of Japan

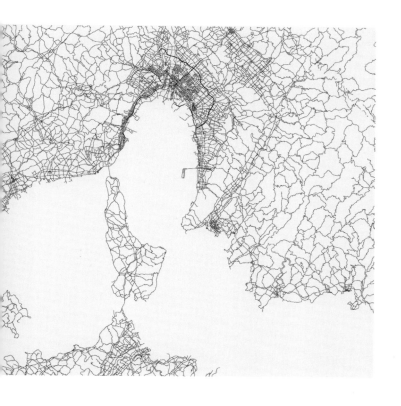

In the Osaka Bay area,
the urban portion is densely developed
with a grid of roads,
while the rivers stretch straight to the bay.

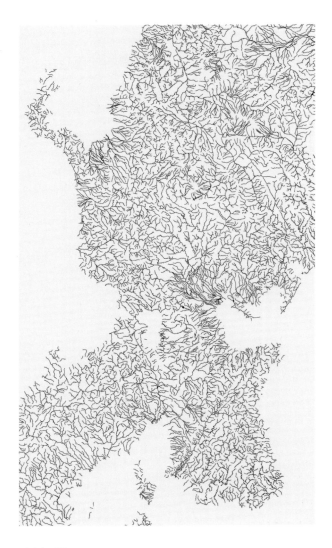

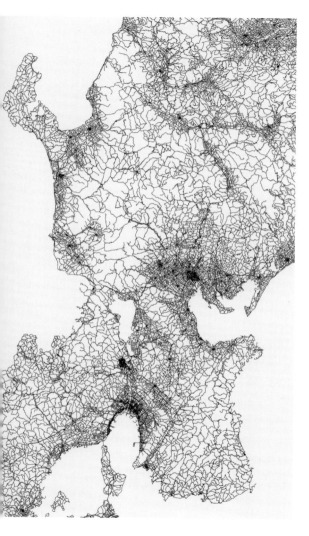

Let's re-perceive
the land of Japan.
The roads run
along the shore,
and trace the
contours of the
archipelago.

4   Pillows

Yuko SATO

Is this the morphology of tension and indentations, or mathematics? A pillow is basically made out of tension. It's a cloth bag sewn into a shape, filled with a voluminous material like cotton, buckwheat chaff, or urethane foam, inflating into a three-dimensional shape. Because it's designed to support a heavy head, it should not only protrude, but ideally also compress. In other words, tension is both the allowance for the act of indenting and the space that guarantees the necessary flexibility for indentation. When a complex three-dimensional figure becomes dented as it supports the shape and weight of a tossing and turning head, naturally it gets wrinkled. If a pillow is for skillfully creating wrinkles to form the ideal indentation, then its most significant elements are indentations and wrinkles, not tension. A single strand of thread attaching the front and back panels limits the pillow's inflation, and the tiniest line of stitching transforms the appearance of both tension and wrinkles. It is intriguing that the interesting variation created by an interweaving of tension, wrinkles, and stitching has given rise to a unique morphological world.

A pillow's construction is simple.
Just sew a cloth bag and fill it with
cotton. Onto this simple tension,
insert wrinkles.

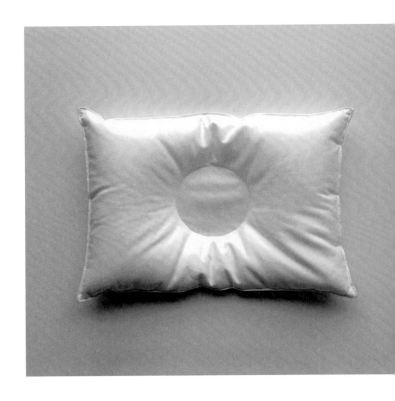

Before filling it with cotton, sew a line
Filling it with cotton gives rise
to both tension and wrinkles.

In the area around the seam,
the puffiness is limited.
The shape of the wrinkles determines
the shape of the pillow.

5 Cast Islands

Tomoko NISHI

Plaster casts of various parts of the hand and arm are placed on a horizontal plane. It's a sight that evokes the illusion of gazing from an airplane over islands in the sea, hence the title. Precise molding accurately reproduces the minute wrinkles of the skin.

By seeing the hand as islands viewed from a distance, shifting the visual scale from microscopic to macroscopic, it's as if we're seeing the hand for the first time, and we revisit our perception, rethinking it.

The protuberance of the palm near the wrist unexpectedly exhibits as a thick lump of flesh. The continuity of the middle joints when the hands are brought together looks like a line of labyrinthine and craggy mountains. The island of the elbow is a rugged rock towering above the sea. And the wrinkles on the surface of the fist thrust into the air look like what a hovering seabird might see, beholding the rock face on which it nests. When we start thinking then about the underwater scene, our imagination runs in dazzling directions. This work is both tranquil and strongly inspirational.

Of all the parts of the human body,
the hand and arm move the most.
To that extent, their wrinkles are
fairly complicated.

Where there are many joints,
there are many wrinkles.
A solitary island sits
amid a placid sea.

A hand appears as islands
floating on the surface of the scene
surveyed by a soaring sea bird.
The hand, and its wrinkles, look like natural terrain.

WRINKLES | Cast Islands

WRINKLES | Cast Islands

WRINKLES | Cast Islands

PLANTS

Plants sometimes look feeble, but in places like dense tropical rainforests they appear ferocious. Their powerful and rampant proliferation could swallow man-made objects like a flood. Something as fragile as a hu seems to need protection.

Are plants strong or weak? They are trampled, cultivated, sheltered, and genetically modified at the whim of human beings. Yet they seem to live as free as the wind under any and all given environments without fighting against our tinkering.

If we assume a century equals a second, trees might appear like firework shot off from the Earth. Each and every one of their leaves leans forward to gather sunlight efficiently. This is what it means to grow rampantly. All moments of vigorous growth are linked, transcending time and taking shape as plants in forests and woods, on grassy plains and fields, and in planters and vases in our homes. The more we deepen our understanding of plants, the more the known truth about them begins to waver. Th series of research is an attempt to release plants into this fluctuation in our cognizance.

1 Overgrown: Plants Are Spreading

Fuyuko KOGI

Shiho SATO

Ayumi NISHIMOTO

These sprouting buds represent the conditions of continual, endless plant growth despite any and all attempts at extermination. At first glance, they look like art, but these are critical works of Ex-formation aimed to make plants unknown. Plants are a tenacious presence; they continue to grow and cover the Earth's surface at an unchangeable pace, whether human beings survive or perish. This team presented one side of plants' nature in a sensational manner. By attaching a great number of buds to the least expected materials and areas, this project conveyed in a striking way the strong and spirited life force of plants, as they grow anywhere.

Plants grow in abundance in Japan, in the temperate monsoon climate zone, but their vitality doubles in tropical regions, where buds will sprout from all kinds of surfaces, like rocks and trees. There are a few that may be free from growth, like glass, metal and plastic, but if they weren't, this is probably what it would look like. This team also did a good job observing how plants grow. The scene is beautiful, yet frightening.

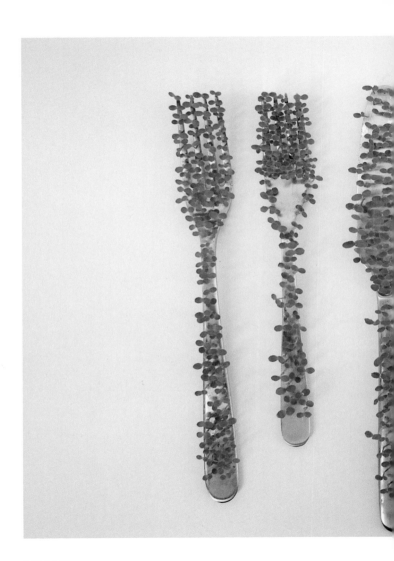

PLANTS | Overgrown: Plants Are Spreading

PLANTS | Overgrown: Plants Are Spreading

PLANTS | Overgrown: Plants Are Spreading

Sprouts run rampant before we know it.
Horror sprouts within the wall clock.
But this is the reality of plants.

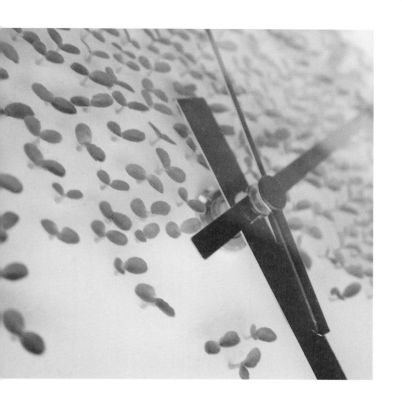

It seems like plants would sprout like this
on chairs left outdoors.
We can't sit here anymore.
It's occupied by plants.

2 Ridges: Agricultural Texture

Asahi ITO

This work is a texture design. This unique texture, originating in scenes of growing produce, calls to the depths of our common perceptions.

From the beginning, Asahi Ito seems to have been conscious of agriculture-related design. In the early stages of the project, he devised correction tape designed to plant "greenery" at regular intervals, like an automatic rice-planting machine. If you lay the tape over part of a document, not only are the offending letters painted white, but little green plantings (as used in architectural models) can also be inserted. The idea was to replace all man-made mistakes with plants. Furthermore, he devised a ridge-like texture reminiscent of real fields by pasting green to the convex part of the corrugated cardboard. It so resembles field scenery that I smile in spite of myself.

Applied to boxes and bags, this texture has a truly mysterious appeal. It is especially charming when produce is loaded inside.

The bottom photo shows a corrugated
cardboard box covered in artificial turf.
These aren't real farm ridges,
but the association comes to mind.

Make a box out of ridges.
Fill it with the harvest.
Vegetables are wrapped
in the fields.

PLANTS | Ridges: Agricultural Texture

Making ridges into bags
isn't particularly ecological.
Perhaps it's psychological.

PLANTS | Ridges: Agricultural Texture

3   Herbivorous

Naoto ENDO

Perishable food is packaged in white Styrofoam trays and wrapped in plastic. This is a truly man-made scene, but nothing special to those of the generation born into this sort of mediated contact with the blessing of nature. They feel the objects are cleaner if presented this way than if displayed on a plate. To those of this generation, mineral water in plastic bottles looks cleaner and safer than water that springs from the ground. To put it the other way around, the packaging itself, a white foam tray wrapped in plastic, has begun to function as an icon indicating *food*.

Our appetite is stimulated by plastic wrap, and from the affixed label we learn the food's name, its meaning, and the expiration date. Observing these circumstances, Naoto Endo presented a line of packaged inedibles: flowers, trees, pine cones, straw, and such. We inadvertently feel our appetite grow for slices of wood, and feel like sprinkling soy sauce on wood shavings.

栃木県産　バラ（橙）

プラ
トレー
ラップ

保存温度 10℃以下

加工年月日	消費期限	品番
20. 1.22	20. 1.28	0003

正味料(g)

100g当り(円)

498

税込価格(円)

2 870109 510018

エクスマート　小平小川店
東京都小平市小川東町 1-6-20

静岡県産　スナゴケ

保存温度 10℃以下

加工年月日	消費期限	品番
20. 1.22	20. 1.28	0026

正味量(g)
371
100g当り(円)
169

627

税込価格(円)

2 870109 510124

エクスマート　小平小川店
東京都小平市小川東町 1-6-20

京都府産　杉（輪切）

保存温度 10℃以下

加工年月日	消費期限	品番
20. 1.22	20. 2. 4	0032

正味料 (g)

100g当り(円)

318

税込価格(円)

2 870109 510117

エクスマート　小平小川店
東京都小平市小川東町 1-6-20

4   Plant that Describes the City

Aya YAMANE

Even if we don't see plants themselves, we feel their presence, as when the shadows of trees fall on buildings. Compared to the shadows of the architecture, clearly thick and motionless, the trees' shadows falling on the concrete walls or stone floors are fluid, constantly murmuring. These shadows wave with the movement of the wind, the light escaping between the leaves perpetually flickering. In concert with its undulations, we feel the wind, and the sunlight. The shadows of trees are a medium through which we feel nature. Normally we aren't clearly conscious of this, but these shadows in the urban space may be the most authentic image of plants that penetrates our sensibilities. The landscape portrayed by Aya Yamane is exactly the view of plants to be found in the city: their intangible shadows swaying to and fro on the surfaces of geometric urban structures. These graphics accurately isolate and present the guise of nature's intermediaries lurking in our deep consciousness.

PLANTS | Plant that Describes The City

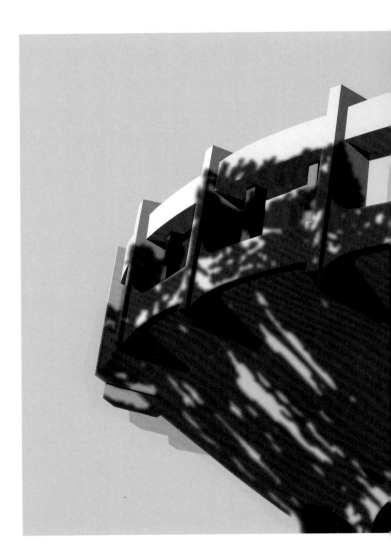

PLANTS | Plant that Describes The City

5 Edges: Unexpected Propagation

Tsugutou FUJIMAKI

Plants grow thick in unexpected crevices. In fact, we may feel the existence of plants most when we witness their propagation in surprising places; moss grows in the gap of a manhole cover, dandelion seeds carried onto tiles germinate and bloom yellow on rooftops; weeds appear between tatami mats in a dilapidated house. This work captures the essence of these plants as books and the typography that develops within.

The letters protruding from the edges of these books impress us strongly with their unpredictability because we expect to see the pages' sharp clean edges. To our further surprise, when we open the book, we find that the protruding letters are parts of sentences.

Having skillfully observed the unique presence of plants, Tsugutou Fujimaki made a unique attempt to apply it to a method of typography which has nothing to do with plants, and in that alone, is highly effective at awakening the viewer.

Every process involved in creating these protruding letters was carried out by hand, in a series of precise work with no intimation of error.

Letters stick out of the edges of the book.
Perhaps the reason that we associate this immediately
with plants is from the memory of plants
flourishing in unusual places.

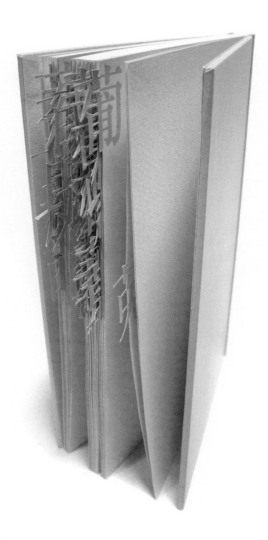

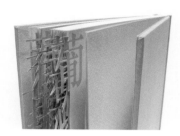

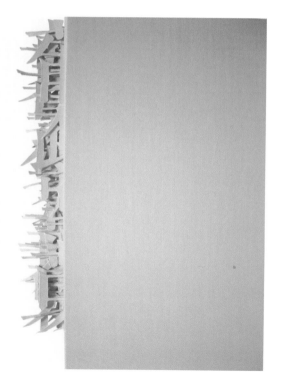

PLANTS | Edges: Unexpected Propagation

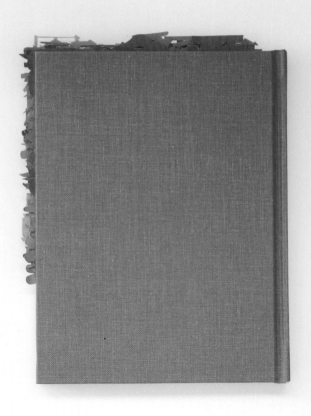

PLANTS | Edges: Unexpected Propagation

6   The Correct Form for a Daikon Radish

Eri SAKUMA
Haruka TAKAHASHI

As the title paradoxically indicates, there has never been an intrinsically correct form for daikon radishes. They aim for the archetypical form, but always evade perfection; in reality, every daikon differs subtly from every other. From this comes a certain narrow view that the distorted daikon that is "correct" precisely because of its irregularity. Cucumbers, whether grown in plastic molds so their shape conforms to kitchen preparation or in pesticide-free soil and deformed as a response to the gnawing of insects, are all still the same cucumbers, each having grown in adaptation to its individual situation.

This team created an idealistic, symmetrical planter, and conjured up imaginary daikon to be grown in it. It's unclear whether or not daikon would grow in it, but through this poetic installation that designates *the correct form for a daikon radish,* a fresh query about plants develops in our minds: "What is the correct form for a daikon?" Who will do a splendid job of uprooting the answer?

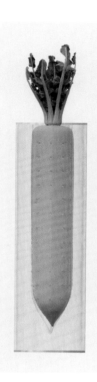

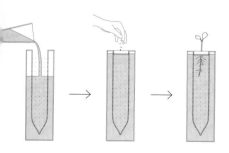

It may look like we're coercing
the plants in some way,
but as far as the plant is concerned,
as long as there's an environment,
it's probably no big deal.

PLANTS | The Correct Form for a Daikon Radish

Here are objects we call "correct daikon."
The question of what is "a correct daikon"
is very freshly sensed from this visual.

You're confused by these visuals.
But it doesn't mean your confusion causes a regression
of your understanding of daikon. On the contrary, having seen these,
you'll focus more carefully on the shape of daikon.

PLANTS | The Correct Form for a Daikon Radish

NUDITY

Why does nudity make us feel shame? And it's not only shame. Without clothes we feel cold; without shoes, we feel pain; and without homes or shelters, we cannot live comfortably. Reconsidering insects, we are amazed by how complete they are, how self-contained. Furry animals also seem stable, although not so much so as insects. Human beings look weak and ephemeral, like jellyfish who've gotten ashore. To that extent, humans endure by devising clothing and shelter to fortify their bare bodies. We also have mysterious inclinations, like feeling sexual urges when seeing someone we find attractive naked, or getting pleasure from a bath.

On the other hand, nudity has produced myriad metaphors. A "naked bike" brings to mind a bicycle without any special accessories; "naked philosophy" conjures an image of ingenious, straightforward thought. It seems that the concept of nudity is peculiar to human beings. We expected to come across some new discoveries when we settled on nudity as a theme and began to attempt to undress it.

1   Materials and Nudity

Kent IITAKA

Junya MAEJIMA

These are very faithful life-sized reproductions of newborn babies. This team covered the surface of the models with various materials and objects: gold leaf, bark, rhinestones, moss and so on. The masterpiece is the flowered baby; the sight of the entire baby covered in dried flowers the size of field poppies or marguerites stuck fast on its skin without an inch to spare evokes a powerful sense of horror; this baby clad in flowers gives an image of death for some reason. With its entire surface, even eyes and mouth, wholly shrouded in flowers, the figure doesn't appear to be alive. Newborn babies are a symbol of nudity. Deep crevices ingrained in their chubby joints, as if they were wearing rubber bands there, fully declare the tender pudginess of their bodies. Oh the pitiful human being, totally defenseless in its infancy and exposed to this world! The sight of those surfaces thickly wrapped in textures is beautiful, yet frightening, acutely recalling for us the fact that human beings exist naked.

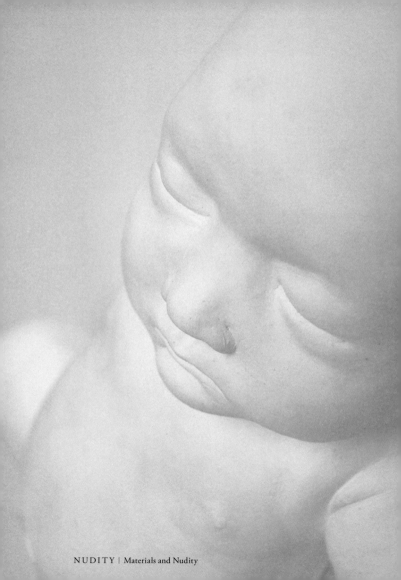

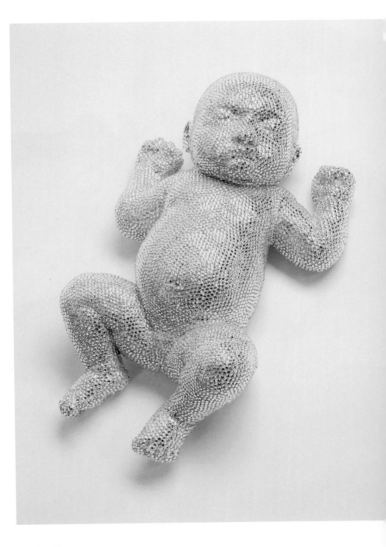

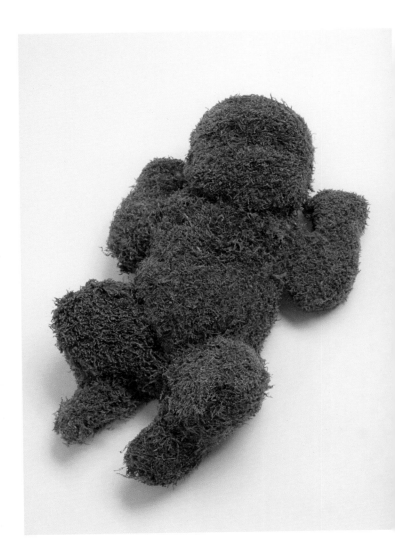

2   Nude Dolls

Kaede ENDO

In this study, special aberrations are added to the bodies of fashion dolls. Fashion dolls' bodies are designed and created as ideal types, but here, the dolls have been granted special physical characteristics, like bowed legs, a stoop, obesity, or an outie belly button. These dolls with their irregularities give one a strangely vivid feeling, and one has to learn how not to stare. The reason we feel shame in nudity is not because we are exposing our skin, but because we resist having our bodies, with their own irregularities, seen by others. The essence of bashfulness surrounding nudity is the exposure of individual abnormalities. So the misshapen fashion doll is a model of the reality of nudity.

Conversely, the act of dressing up is one of obscuring our individual peculiarities. Ultrathin leotards that completely cover the skin but also perfectly reveal the body's lines are close to nudity. This study does a marvelous job of pointing out and expressing the truth about nudity viewed in this context.

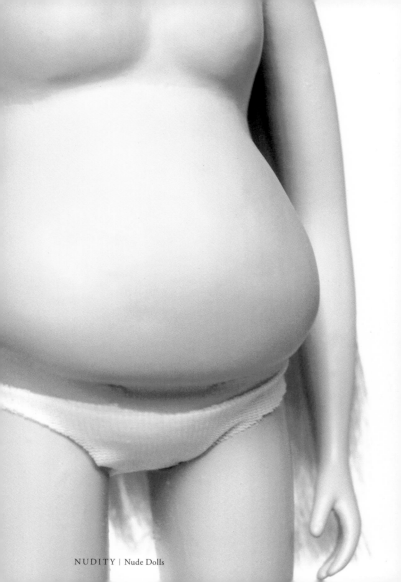

NUDITY | Nude Dolls

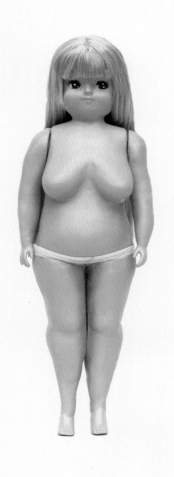

NUDITY | Nude Dolls

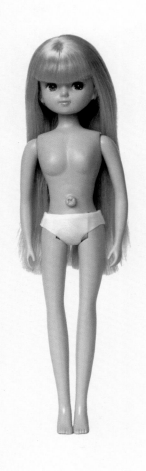

NUDITY | Nude Dolls

3   Undies Project

Sachie MURAKAMI

For this project, the team dressed various objects in underpants and took photos. The material is a high-tech jersey knit, which stretches but doesn't fray. The undies approach makes the object appear as a body, achieving visual personification. By cladding a thing in undies, hips miraculously appear to the viewer and the object dramatically takes on physicality. The piman pepper with its sexy twists; the nail puller that makes you feel its supple flexibility; the egg, with a body more plump and luxurious than any human's; the mini tomato... all elicit spontaneous smiles. They feel so familiar: the drinking fountain faucet in the park appears divine, like Venus. We even feel a sense of affinity with the clothespin flawlessly wearing its undies. There is nothing left to say. This project is the most responsive answer to the Ex-formation approach. Undies make the world nude.

NUDITY | Undies Project

NUDITY | Undies Project

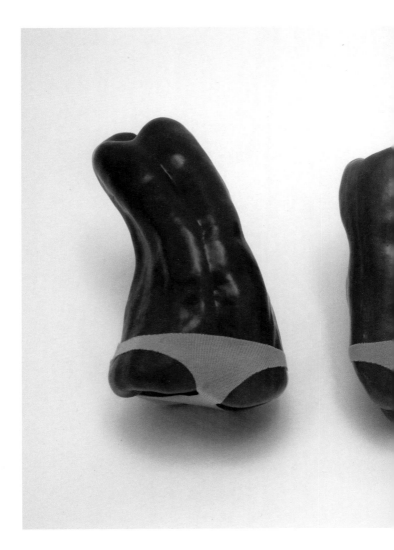

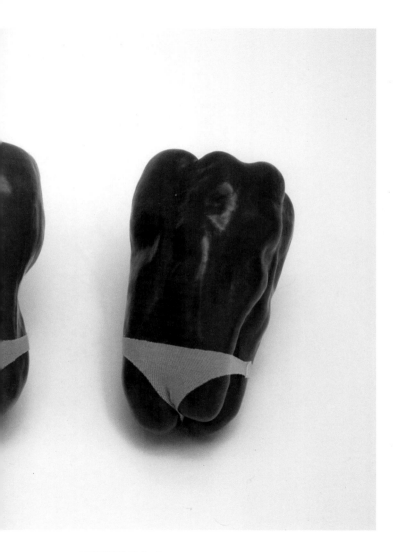

NUDITY | Undies Project

4 Undressing *Completion*

Eriko TAKAYANAGI

This project expresses the charm of products before they're finished. Unfinished parts make one feel the distinct air of materiality, and seeing them somehow makes one feel *nudity*. The viewpoint of this research is perceptive and unique. The top of a pull-tab beer can, freshly pressed car hoods, a big pile of mobile phone bodies just released from the mold: we are strangely struck by processing and material each time we encounter these kinds of scenes, and harbor strange emotions about the reality of material civilization. Eriko Takayanagi has grasped a nuance that can be called *nudity*, and which cannot be felt from these products when they are finished. By no means do Takayanagi's products demonstrate the intermediate stage of production; you could call it the *antecedent* phase rather than en route. That is, it is an intentional deviation from completion. The moment we realize that they are not the form of mid-production, we are mired in her magic.

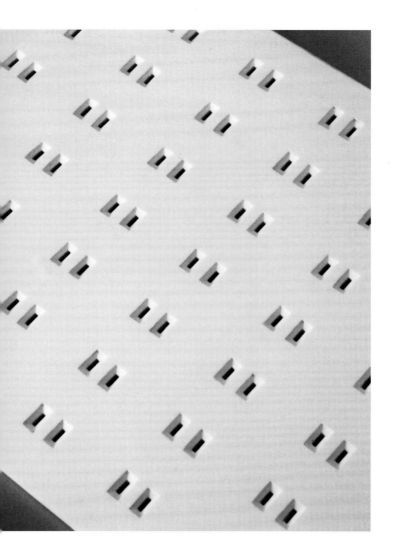

NUDITY | Undressing *Completion*

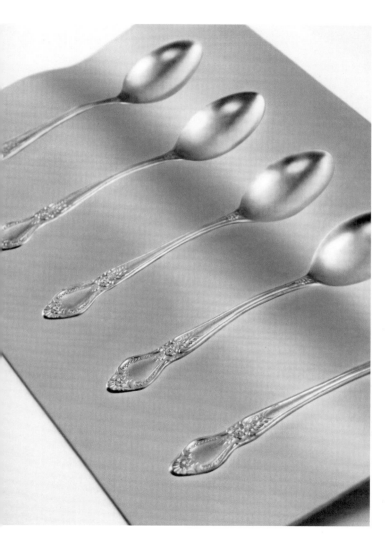

NUDITY | Undressing *Completion*

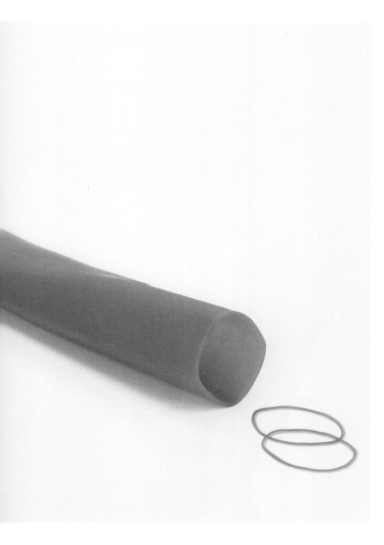

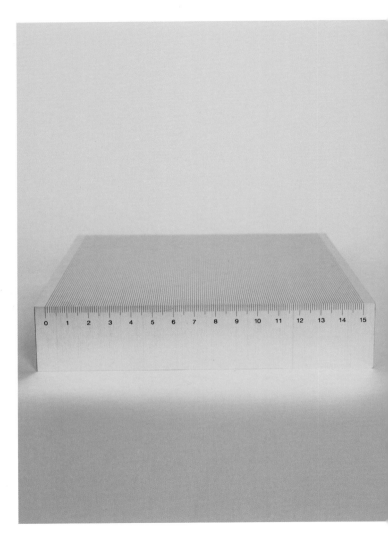

NUDITY | Undressing *Completion*

5 Buttocks

Kota FUJIKAWA
Aya FUNAKI

Kids love butts; the minute they see a bottom, they react immediately, laughing and making merry. Why is this?

The human bottom is a pair of bulges sheltering a single chasm between them. There are arranged the functions of excretion and reproduction. Perhaps since both are important functions related to the survival of life, they are stored deep in the valley, protected by pliable fatty tissue. Maybe because it's a place where such important functions are stored, people are particularly aware of it, resulting, perhaps, in a very strong power of attraction and affinity. This research focused on buttocks, applying molding to various objects, realizing a design with a strange charm. This is surely buttocks application design. Every single one draws a laugh, tiles and building blocks, castanets and marshmallows, sugar cubes and matches.... The buttocks exhibit a special allure that can attract people's attention.

NUDITY | Buttocks

NUDITY | Buttocks

Wooden blocks: Play with the cleft between the
buttocks and the rounded parts. Unexpected discoveries
arise from the various sequences and combinations.

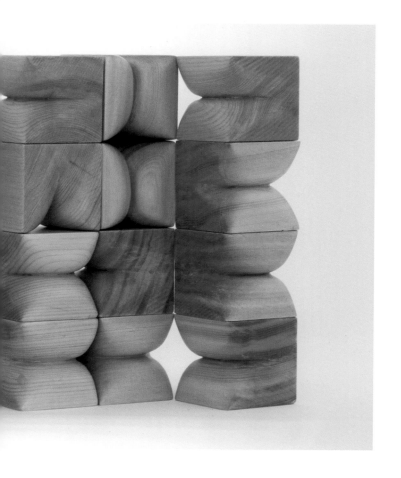

NUDITY | Buttocks

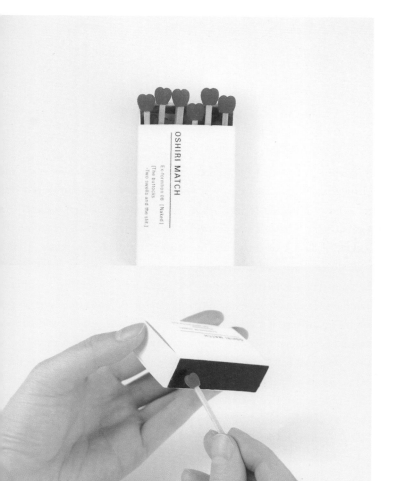

OSHIRI MATCH

Ex-formation 08 [Naked]

[The buttocks
-Two swells and the slit.]

NUDITY | Buttocks

WOMAN

According to Claude Lévi-Strauss, women were the objects of trade and gift-giving. When a man gives a woman to another man, it puts a stop to incest, and leads to fertility or the prosperity of descendants. An arrangement in which a man owns a large number of women more efficiently leads to prosperity than the other way around. Therefore, women were gifted, and symbolized prosperity. In today's society, characterized by monogamous relationships, gender equality is becoming a matter of common sense, and we see rapid changes in social awareness about gender. Women's suffrage is a topic of the distant past, the systems and climate around advocacy for women's rights and position go too far, to the point that "reverse discrimination" has become a problem. No longer are there exhortations to "act like a man" or "act like a woman." The individual is left to his or her own nature. In this project, the students threw off the shackles of cultural anthropology and biology, and reexamined woman. With an overview of the various ways women exist today, we want to take a fresh look at *woman* as the reproductive gender.

1   People who Give Birth

Female is the gender that conceives. Yuka Okazaki devised and implemented a unique method to make the viewer reexamine this unequivocal
difference between the genders. Although the researcher costumed her
self as many different types of woman, every one of them is pregnant.
One might think that it's not very difficult to disguise oneself as pregnant, but it is. Also, when you think about it, there probably isn't another
country in which there exist such a diversity of appearances for women.
Even among women of the same age, there's a vast variety, from goth,
Loli* types to the kimono type; from those who like cosplay** to pro
fessional golfers. Looking at row upon row of these images of a woman
disguised as various expectant mothers is deeply moving. From the fac
that one woman is playing all these roles we can understand directly the
possibility that one woman can become any of them. And all of them are
pregnant. Because of the disguises, we are reminded of Cindy Sherman
or Yasumasa Morimura. This is a precise and ingenious critical work that
compares favorably to that of those artists.

*goth/Loli: Essentially, this is a fusion of gothic and Lolita, a Japan-specific fashion style, or subculture
characterized by clothing that centers on blacks and whites, and presents a darker, more elegant Lolit
style. **cosplay: This term blends costume and role play, describing the practice of dressing up and
pretending to be a character from entertainment media.

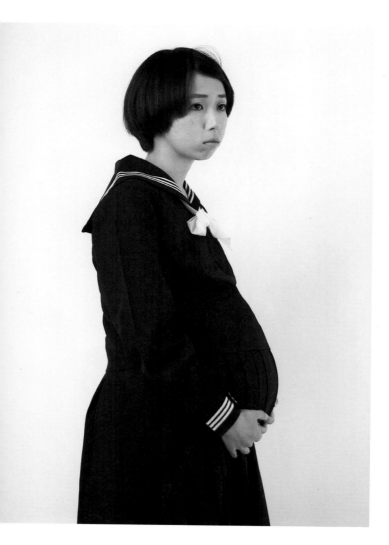

WOMAN | People who Give Birth

WOMAN | People who Give Birth

WOMAN | People who Give Birth

WOMAN | People who Give Birth

WOMAN | People who Give Birth

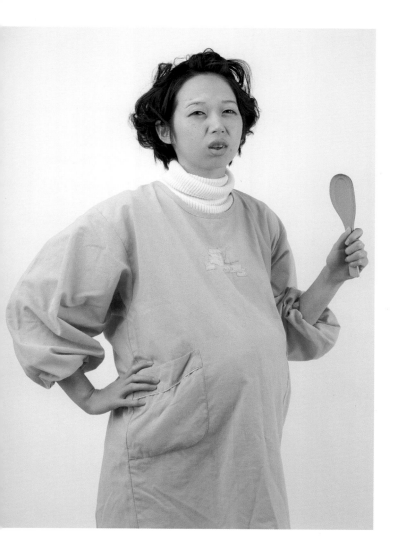

WOMAN | People who Give Birth

2   Lovely Ware

Megumi KAWAGOE
Yu KAWANA
Eriko FUJII

Weapons are covered with a floret print pattern. In a work of this kind, the finesse and degree of perfection exhibited in realizing it is even more important than the uniqueness of the concept; by doing it thoroughly and with determination, this team succeeded in meeting—or exceeding—its intentions. First, we shudder at the floral missile. This is not an antiwar political message. Having said that, it's also not a sexy tease, like, "My missile's made a direct hit on your heart." Exclusively covered in a floral pattern are a missile, a machine gun and bullets, hand grenades, and a gas mask. Looking at these perfectly made objects, we are just perplexed and embarrassed, as we sense that the icon of the floret print, which cloaks these weapons, nonetheless has the effect of softening the surroundings generously and genially, which in the end rather subtly amplifies the reality of war and slaughter.

WOMAN | Lovely Ware

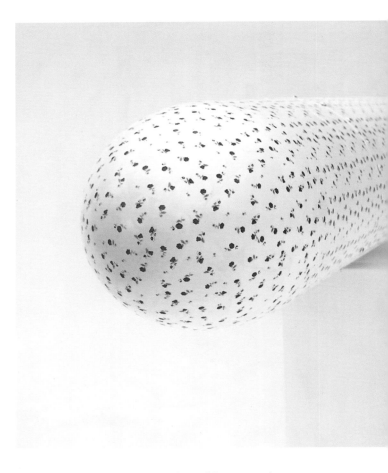

Gas mask (previous page)
and actual-size cruise missile

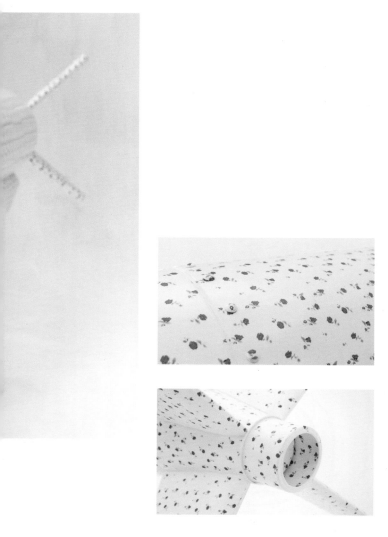

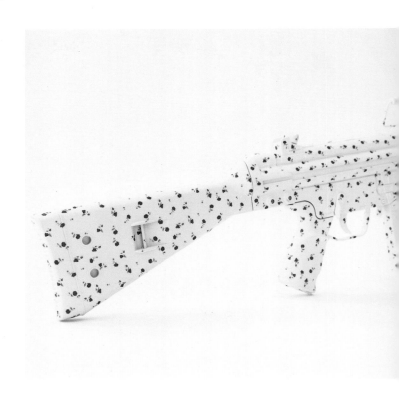

Actual-size machine gun and ammo
Next spread: grenades
The flowers are not an anti-war message.

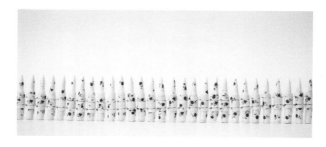

WOMAN | Lovely Ware

WOMAN | Lovely Ware

3 Flora

Asuka TADA

Asuka Tada made skeletons that looked like X-ray images made out o
pressed flowers. This is a duplicate image combining pressed flower
and an X-ray image of bones. I don't know what Tada's inspiration wa
for intuitively linking these two, but the translucency or permeability o
pressed flowers certainly resembles that of X-ray images. However, th
relentless passion necessary to construct an entire skeleton out of colorfu
pressed flowers is unusual. The coexistence of beauty and death, flam
boyance and gravity, has a deep emotional impact on viewers.

Once, in *The Book of Tea*, Tenshin Okakura stated that if there were n
such thing as flowers, human beings would certainly be destitute, in bot
life and death. This very well might be so. Through their special signif
icance, flowers support our lives and our deaths. That same intuition i
in Tada's work, which evokes some strange nostalgia that circulates, vi
aesthetic sensibility, in both flowers and women, life and death.

WOMAN | Flora

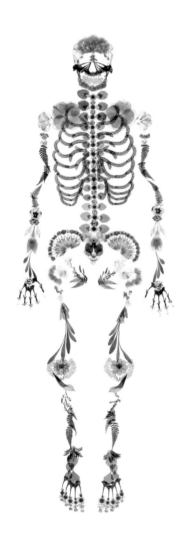

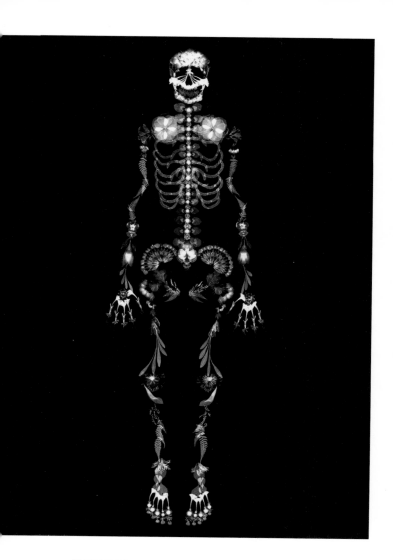

WOMAN | Flora

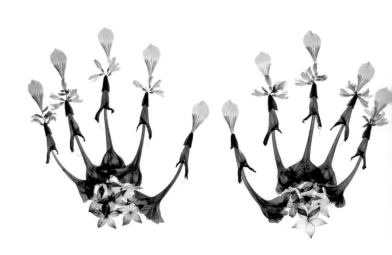

WOMAN | Flora

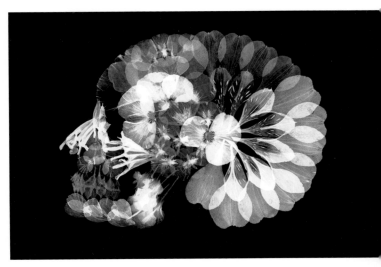

WOMAN | Flora

WOMAN | Flora

4   Nice Body PET Bottles

Keisuke NAKANO

Keisuke Nakano attempts to grasp woman from the symbolism of the form of the female body. Some exemplary female body shapes are: Japanese anime's grotesque sensual forms, with their pinched waists; Botticelli's *Venus*; the substantial and plump clay figurines from ancient burial grounds; the hefty bodies of Botero's drawings and Harunobu Suzuki's ukiyoe female beauties, slim and willow-waisted. The infantility of child anime characters also includes femininity. Keisuke Nakano abstracted this femininity in the form of PET bottles. By reflecting the female body this way, Nakano is trying to create a target of consciousness that draws our attention the way clay figurines or Botero's women and Marilyn Monroe do. Certainly, some of the images have the allure to arouse interest

B 32
W 36
H 36

Venus of Willendorf

WOMAN | Nice Body PET Bottles

B 17
W 12
H 20

From Triptych of Earthly Vanity
and Divine Salvation:
Oil painting by Hans Memling

ION SUPPLY DRINK

POCARI
SWEAT

POCARI SWEAT is a healthy beverage that smoothly supplies the lost water and electrolytes during perspiration. With the appropriate density and electrolytes, close to that of human body fluid, it can be easily absorbed into the body.

B 23
W 18
H 24

Miwa Asao
(Former beach volleyball player/athlete)

B 15
W 13
H 15

From the Mistress of Kurofuneya:
Woodblock print by Yumeji Takehisa

B 21
W 12
H 24

Female character Fujiko Mine
from T Vanime Lupin III

WOMAN | Nice Body PET Bottles

B 18
W 14
H 20

From the Birth of Venus
By Sandro Botticelli

B 12
W 8
H 12
───────────
Betty Boop

4 Woman's Poker Face

Kiyoe KOBAYASHI

The genders are raised in society being told things like, "Men have cour age, women have charm." Possibly because of this, women smile a lo The woman's smiling face is expected to be part of service, and wome are trained accordingly. A smiling face is created through training. Th applies to the smiles of females in all walks of life: flight attendants, foo restaurant employees, TV personalities, nurses. Of course this connectic with a good impression is not confined to women; men can smile to mal a good impression, too. In Japan, the saying, "Men should not show the teeth" is no longer uttered in training male youth.

However, to the extent that there's nothing strange about a man wh doesn't smile, men and smiling are not conjoined. But what if we were remove smiling from women? At the food counter, at the bank windo in airplane seats, people might feel chilled by the countenance of a no smiling woman. Through reductio ad absurdum (proof through contr diction) these nonsmiling women rendered in pencil drawings throw in stark relief the societal connection between women and smiling.

WOMAN | Woman's Poker Face

WOMAN | Woman's Poker Face

WOMAN | Woman's Poker Face

6   Stick Figures

Anri YAMADA

Stick figures appear in flip books, simple sketches of people with a roun head and a torso, arms and legs drawn as lines. Naturally, they have neithe facial expressions nor elaborate physical characteristics. There is also n expression of gender difference. With this work, in which the blank-face stick figure is animated, the viewer senses the explicitly female maneuver ability and actions of the character. Because the stick figure, its physica characteristics completely erased, is a pure medium, if woman can b sensed from the animation, it means that the salvaged content is pure physical information that is certainly recognized in society as *woman* This is just a simple piece, and all the more for that reason, Anri Yamada work confronts us with woman in society, offering intense criticism by wa of an enlightening disclosure. People who look at this work may laug unintentionally, but within that laugh is profound empathy toward woman. I really hope that people appreciate this movie.

Scan the QR code
to watch the animation.

The stick figure demonstrates a girl's running gait.
In Japan, everybody who sees this animation laughs.
At least in our country, this action is recognized
as the way women run.

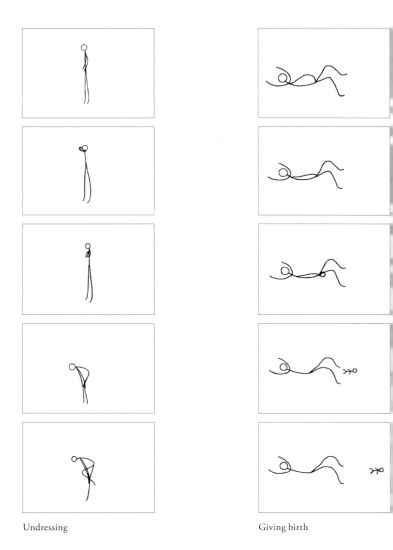

Undressing

Giving birth

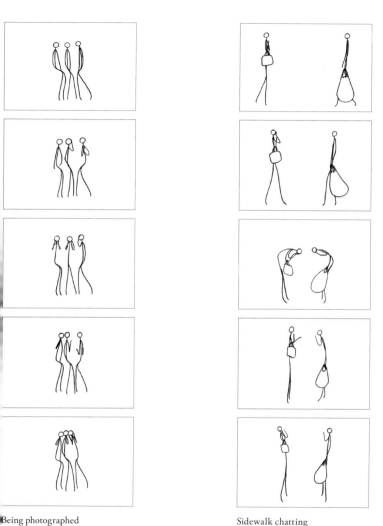

Being photographed

Sidewalk chatting

HALF-DONE

The world is at a turning point. Everything is in a mutable state, facing great changes: energy production methods and consumption efficiency, automatic operation-based transfer and transportation, the models for services based on sensing and analyzing big data, the value of agricultural output, the structure of industries focused on food and tourism/lodging, and the structure of families and the way housing is built. We must all step down from our current positions in society, stand at ground zero, figure out what kind of contribution we can make to society and reexamine what kind of compensation we will take for the contribution we make: presidents and poets, investors and professional wrestlers, police officers and real estate appraisers, designers and bakers. The resources for creating affluence lie in our ability to identify a value in our work for which there is no substitute.

The following words came out of our discussion about *half-done*: soft boiled, incomplete, immature, undefined, ambiguous, enroute, mutable, green, half baked and translucent. If we face these head on, I wonder what we'll find.

1   Ladybirds

Eriko AKATA

This research pursued the possibilities of ladybird patterns. This is a challenge to nature. Generally speaking, people probably know that ladybirds are cute insects with black-spotted red shells. I expected that there were variations in the patterns on their smooth round wings, but both I and the other members of the seminar had thought there wouldn't be very many possible variations. However, when I saw the wild proliferation of patterns in Eriko Akata's work, I began to worry. I thought that the breadth of her research would generate too many variations, eventually surpassing the sphere of living organisms. I advised her to have an entomology researcher look at it and give an opinion. Unexpectedly, the expert did not repudiate any possibilities. The pairs of ladybirds with different markings continually produced descendants whose patterns sometimes came to resemble one another's, yet sometimes they produced completely different markings, constantly changing. It has become clear that the patterns of the ladybird are en route, never settling.

HALF-DONE | Ladybirds

HALF-DONE | Ladybirds

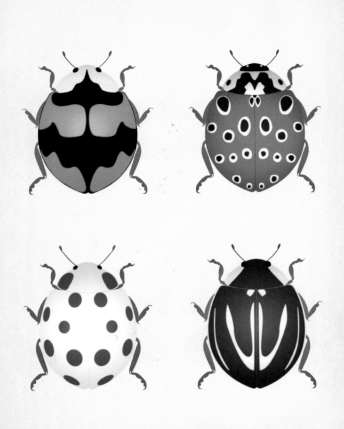

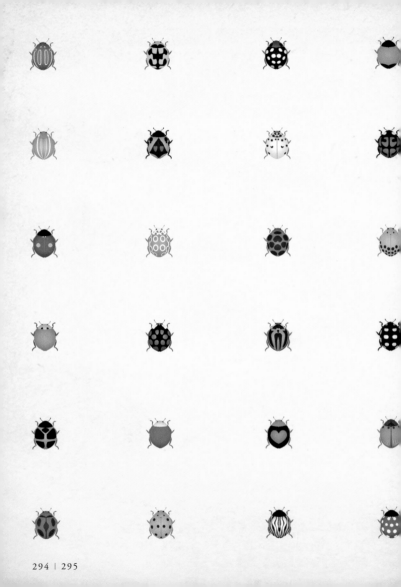

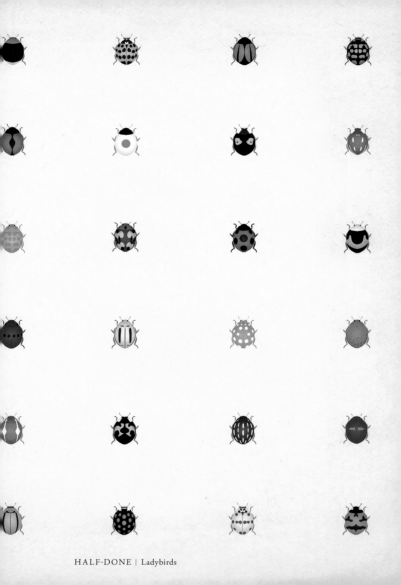

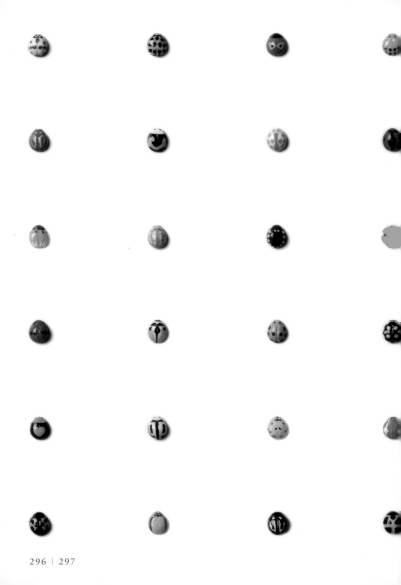

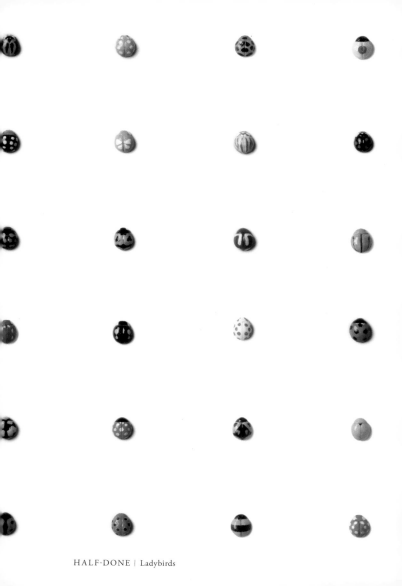

HALF-DONE | Ladybirds

2   Before Baked

Midori YAMAMOTO
Sari YUKAWA

The moist dough of a loaf of bread before it's baked has a strong attractive power for the human senses. Perhaps our interest is aroused by that air of moistness when the dough still holds water, that still-tender, midway state, full of possibility. Baked bread, whose color and hardness have both stabilized, has the presence of a finished product, but the charm of bread dough is lost. Bread shares this trait with porcelain and other materials: the application of heat and high temperatures stabilizes the material. However, the antecedent state, the *before baked* form, continually transmits the possibility of allowing for any and all change. For some reason bread, porcelain, and other such materials also share a pale beige tone, not yet attaining an unbridled expression of color.

This team of two named this charming essence *before baked*, and mostly used photos to seek it out and analyze it. Within the series of processes they undertook were various steps: observation, understanding, application; steps also followed in the process of setting trends or fashion to put a value system into practice. This team has simulated these processes using the value system called *before baked*, and showed us the results of its implementation.

HALF-DONE | Before Baked

HALF-DONE | Before Baked

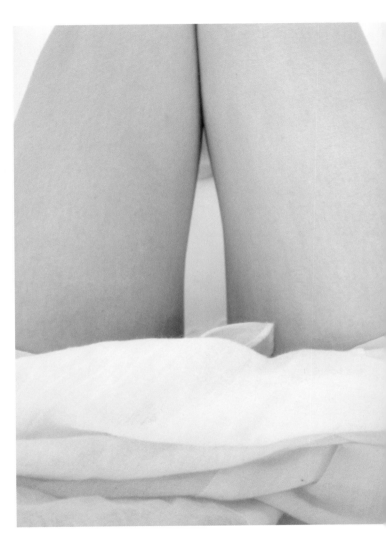

HALF-DONE | Before Baked

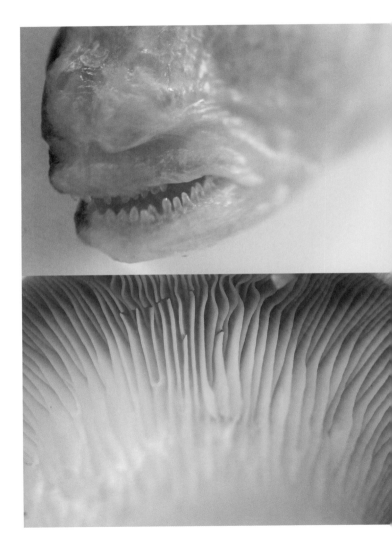

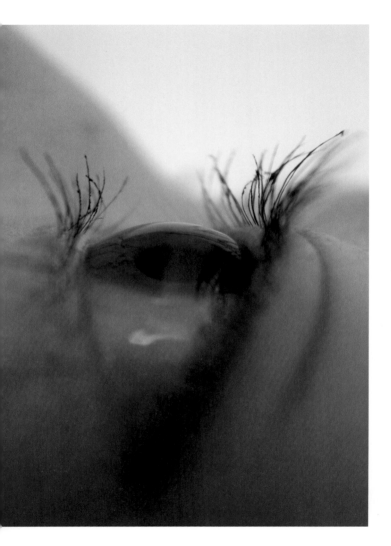

HALF-DONE | Before Baked

3   Stuffed Toys

Katsuya YAMAMOTO

I sympathized with the sincere attitude underlying this research, i
which Yamamoto attempted to look into and analyze the unique feature
of stuffed toys in a critical manner, instead of just presenting them as cut
and adorable.

Most of the time was spent gathering data and case studies, but amon
those, one pair of stuffed toys caught the eye; one looked like a dissecte
frog, and the other, a dissected rat. The nuance of the stretched skin an
the gentle internal organs was so skillfully, realistically, and humorousl
duplicated that it was surprising. The use of soft wool allowed for ger
erous deformation, perfectly capturing the essence of the subjects. Ther
were smiles on the toys' faces, but therein lay clever communication. Ya
mamoto calmly observed this, and implemented it by creating a stuffed to
of a specific object.

That's how The Bankroll Toy came to be. Yamamoto learned the rule
through observation, and followed them precisely in his implementatio
This is an admirable piece of research.

HALF-DONE | Stuffed Toys

HALF-DONE | Stuffed Toys

HALF-DONE | Stuffed Toys

HALF-DONE | Stuffed Toys

4   Cast-off Skin / Second Birth

Natsumi TOYODA

This research began with an interest in photographs of development through molting. Certainly our eyes are unwittingly drawn to the sight of an insect emerging from its chrysalis as an imago, or adult. If we happen upon the scene of a molting cicada, every one of us is drawn in, with hushed breath. The insect comes into this world with translucent whitish body and wings, still delicate and soft. It is also completely defenseless, and there would be nothing it could do if it were attacked, but it solemnly carries on with its molting, giving off an air of some sort of resignation. Natsumi Toyoda has reproduced this enticement in line drawings. Delicate lines and pale colors skillfully communicate the reality of molting. As she went on, the work began to develop into fictional drawings of moltings: an elephant, a seahorse, a bat, even a person. A strange thought came to mind: All living creatures undergo transformation by way of metamorphosis and molting.

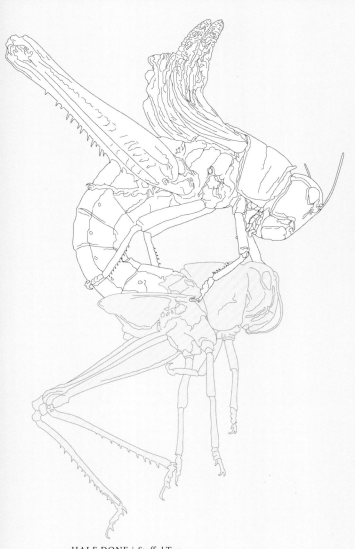

HALF-DONE | Stuffed Toys

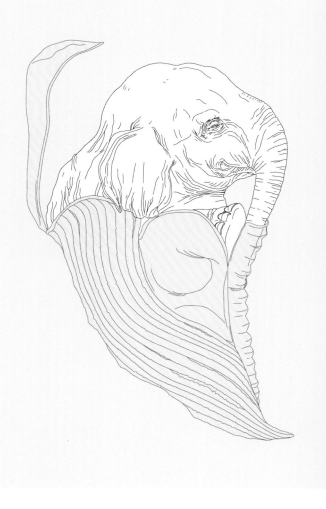

HALF-DONE | Stuffed Toys

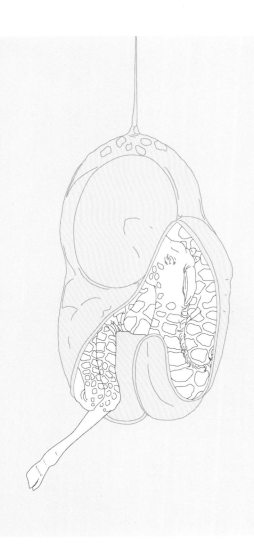

HALF-DONE | Stuffed Toys

HALF-DONE | Stuffed Toys

5   Obscure

Megumi NISHINA

Photos of UFOs, photos of Nessie, photos of the yeti and of aliens..
photos of all dubious objects share common features: every one is grainy
the subject is fuzzy, out of focus. If the Nessie photo were a little mor
distinct, presumably it would be possible to clarify whether this is a rea
elasmosaurus or a fake, or a mistake involving another photographic subject
But these photos are invariably blurred.

Nishina was interested in these kinds of photos and began by collectin
them. As she catalogued them, a trend became clear. As long as the subject
remained in a state of questionability, in which their authenticity wa
ambiguous, the photos would excite people's interest and curiosity. B
leaving a vague, indefinite component, there is room into which to invit
people's attention and concern. Having grasped this tendency, Nishin
used a pinhole camera to take ambiguous photos and achieved a metho
of creating "soft-boiled" photos.

t is difficult to discern forms or
details in old photos, black and white
photos and those taken at dawn or
dusk.

ttp://www.nationalgeographic.
o.jp/
ttp://spacejay.com/

his has been said to be a U F O,
ut it might also appear to be
cloud.
ardly limited to clouds,
ings shot casually at the edge
f the field of vision often appear to
e something completely different.

tp://spacejoy.com/Evidence/
fo-Fotos/Ufo-Fotos-01.htm

HALF-DONE | Obscure

HALF-DONE | Obscure

AIR

If humans were as small as ants, we might fly through the air. I recall a number of sketches I made on the chalkboard when we were talking about this. The shapes were of something billowed by air; something swayed by air; bubbles rising to the surface of the water; two-bladed propellers spiraling through the air; dandelion fluff floating; the movement of a dragonfly, whose mechanism can not be discerned by the naked eye; jet propulsion, and so on.

We were also inspired by the image of an elderly person making a giant soap bubble. The figure, armed with solemnity and a unique dignity, exactly in the way that the Creator or a pastor manipulates air, continued to make a whale-grade soap bubble on the beach. It was an indescribably happy sight.

The students' sensibility is indeed unrestrained and responsive. They go going, surpassing the imagery I had presented. Due to the explosive expansion of the artistic frontier brought by technology since the arrival of the computer, it seems as if the world is rapidly changing, but I believe that what really changes the world is the human imagination, which, apprehending change, mobilizes and expands.

1   Undulations

Aoi MORIYA

A stream of smoke from a stick of incense rises up, immediately stirring, responding to the slightest waver in the air. As the solid white smoke rises up from the burning incense, it gets close to the oscillating air, and finally, as if swallowed by the atmosphere, the smoke from the incense will diffuse and disappear. It reminds us of the flow path of consciousness which mediates between this world and the hereafter. In the movement of the medium, smoke, which precisely traces the fluctuations in invisible gas, people are brought close to the feeling of prayer. This research, focusing on the smoke from incense, attempts to express its wavering form with molded incense sticks. The concept is interesting, but I worried if Aoi Moriya could realize it in any way. However, she came up with a method by which she stuffed soft, kneaded incense into a needle-less syringe and extruded it, expressing it as a solid. The products also resemble smoke in that no two have the same shape. She took great care with her products, each of which is placed in a paulownia box,* presenting a tenderly cared for collection of individualistic undulations.

*Paulownia wood, traditionally used for incense boxes, keeps the humidity at a specific level.

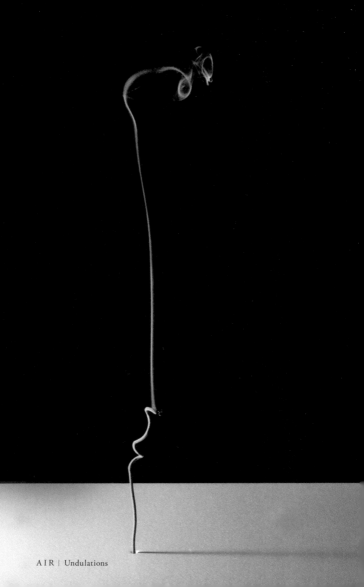

AIR | Undulations

AIR | Undulations

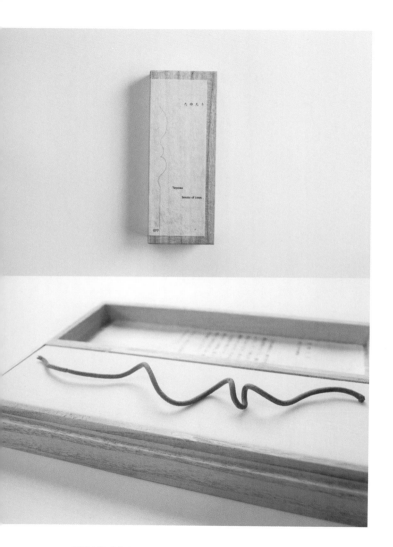

AIR | Undulations

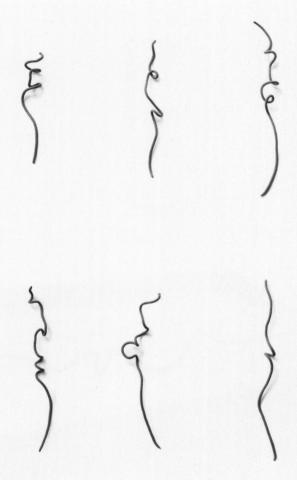

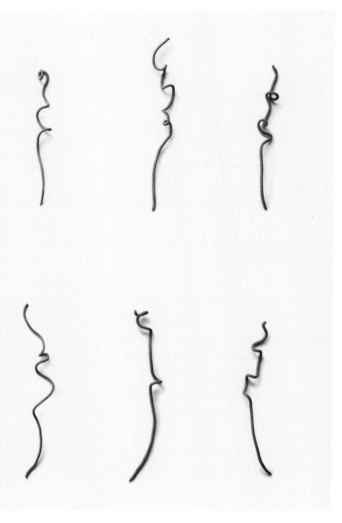

2   Wearing the Bulge

Akane ONUKI

At first, Akane Onuki, thinking it be would good to feel the air in a husk or cast-off skin, made the husks of really familiar things. Although the concept is understandable, if the familiar object is not a living thing, but rather something like a coin or a mobile phone, no matter how well you might form its husk out of some translucent material, not only will there be no traces of life, but you also won't come near the reality of something that's been shed. Therefore, it won't appear as a slough or husk. Through trial and error, Onuki arrived at "Wearing the Bulge" as her theme.

I thought it interesting that, unlike the concept of ordinary clothes, she had the idea to create one more layer, a body-like bulge, to apply to the outside of the body. I was really worried about whether or not she would be able to make a three-dimensional object out of vinyl, a material that's hard to work with, but this turned out to be a teacher's needless anxiety. Onuki did a magnificent job, using thermocompression techniques and transparent vinyl to create an object with a body-like bulge. There are interesting inferences to be made from things like the choice of the nipple as the location for the air inlets.

AIR | Wearing the Bulge

AIR | Wearing the Bulge

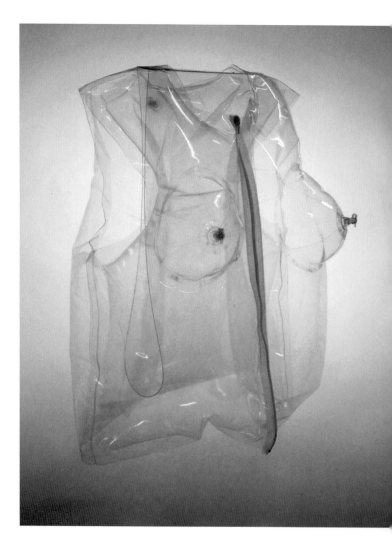

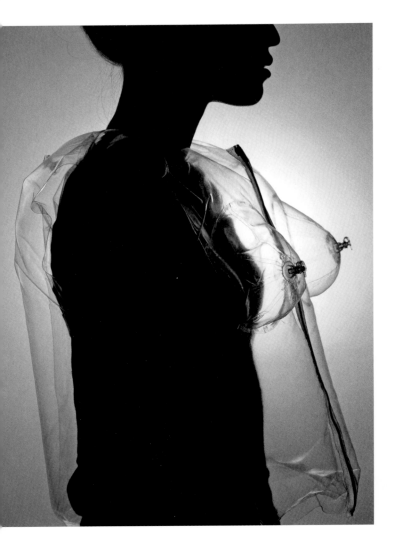

AIR | Wearing the Bulge

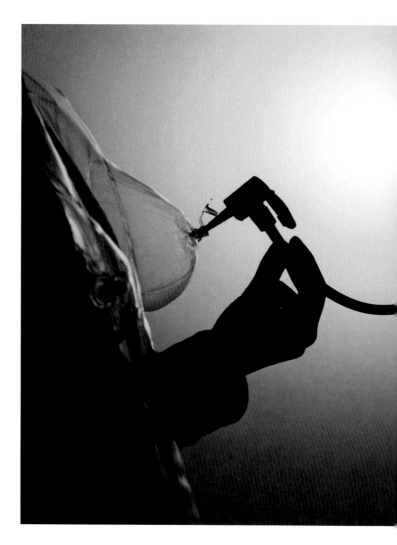

A I R | Wearing the Bulge

AIR | Wearing the Bulge

3   Holes

This is research into the shapes of holes. The shape of a hole change depending on what will go in or come out of it. Will delicate insects g in and out? Will air or smoke flow through? Will liquids or acoustics pas through? We see geometrically arrayed holes around the speakers for elec trical equipment, and from experience imagine that sound will come ou of them. What things flow through what kinds of openings? Seiji Tahar used an eggshell as a basis for presenting a collection of holes. Because a egg is a fortress for the storage of life, it's a big deal if it gets a hole in it Therefore, our consciousness is adroitly alerted to detect holes in an egg Organic holes made by ants that signal an erosion of life; geometric, man made holes; closely packed homogenous holes; a gaping hole as if a wal has been removed.... This work, making us tremble in horror at the var ious holes in the surfaces of these eggshells, also makes us acutely awar of the meaning of holes.

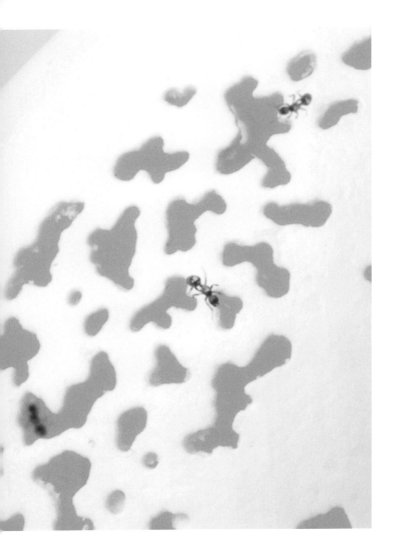

AIR | Holes

AIR | Holes

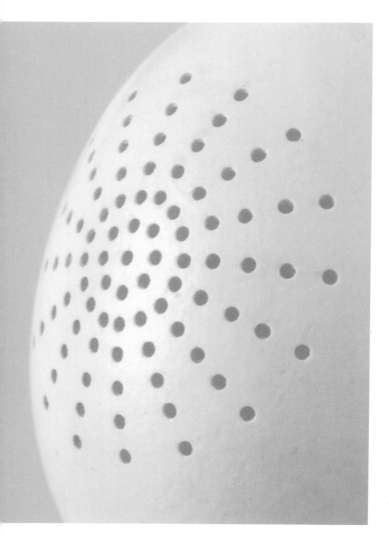

A I R | Holes

AIR | Holes

4 Windows: Looking through the Air

Maki OTA

Maki Ota's interest in windows began with her research. She replaced the monitor of her clamshell mobile phone with a piece of transparent plastic, allowing a view of the other side. It looked like either a tool with new function or futuristic communication equipment whose application is as yet unknown. Pretending to take a call, when she put the phone to her ear, it appeared in the transparent "window," giving me a strange futuristic sensation. A window gives a frame to the world of infinity, and a frame defines context and meaning.

Before long, Ota began to open square windows in other things: potato chips, loaves of bread, cookies, blocks of tofu, sugar cubes and so on. From several of these holes began streaming a breath of fresh air. Potato chip windows seemed to have been made for diets, while the window piercing the bread gave the impression of a hole, rather than a window. Toasted slices of the bread, their interiors also browned, expressed a mysterious poetic sentiment.

AIR | Windows: Looking through the Air

5 Depth: Expression through Shadows

Kinuko OHSHIMA

Chie SAKAKURA

Shogo MORI

This team's research focuses on grasping space by using shadows instead of substance to express movement and buoyancy, and to try to represent the depth of the space in which they are placed. In shallow water filled with light, fish silhouettes are seen on the bottom. Big fish cast sluggishly moving shadows, while the agile and delicate shadows of a school of small fish drop to the bottom. From their shadows, we recognize their mobility and buoyancy, rather than the forms of the fish themselves. Shadows of something like a group of sea lice nimbly crawling about a rocky area (or perhaps a colony of cockroaches), swarming on and crawling over the ground, are some of the numerous wonders of life, but also fill us with a sensation of horror. The silhouette of a black kite or a hawk, its wings spread wide, makes us feel as if we are looking down over its flight from high up in the skies above, creating an illusion of depth, as if there were several hundred meters of vertical space between us. In complete contrast, we feel the presence of the water's surface from the shadow of ripples or the sight of dried leaves falling there. The continually edited photographs ingeniously grasp the very air and its depth.

AIR | Depth: Expression through Shadows

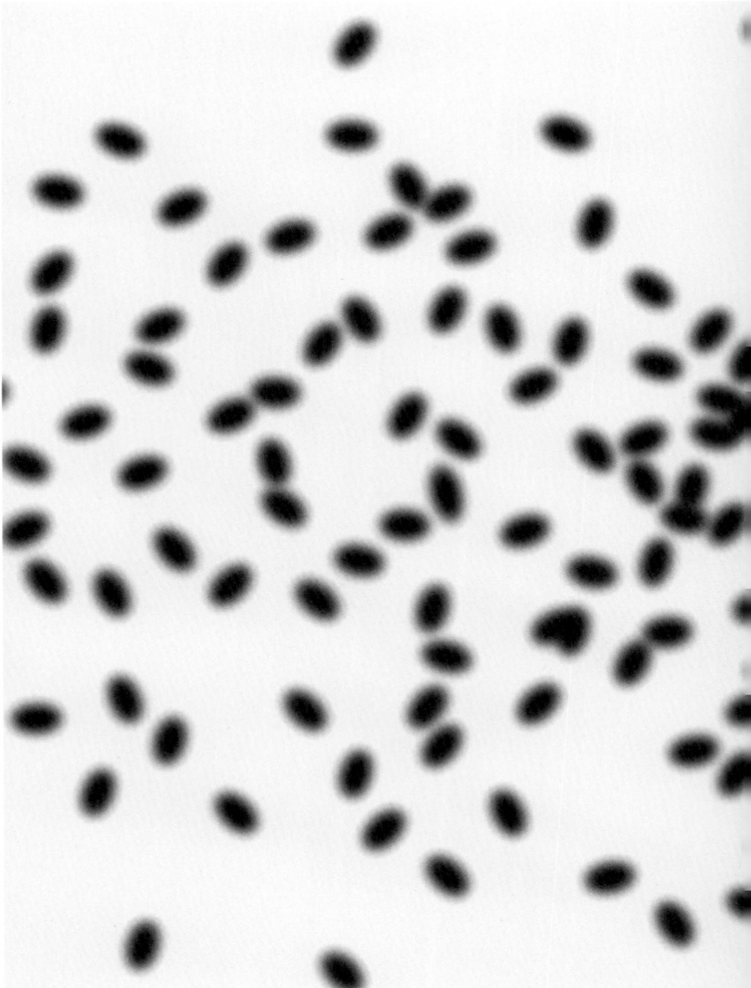

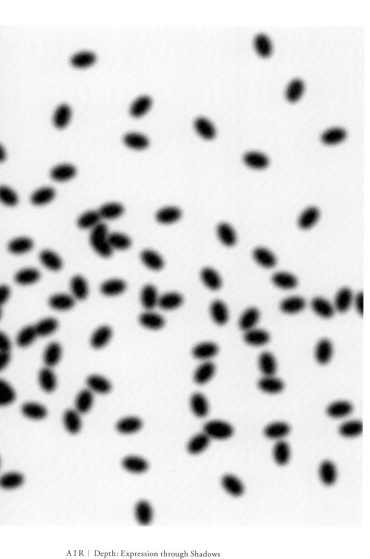

AIR | Depth: Expression through Shadows

AIR | Depth: Expression through Shadows

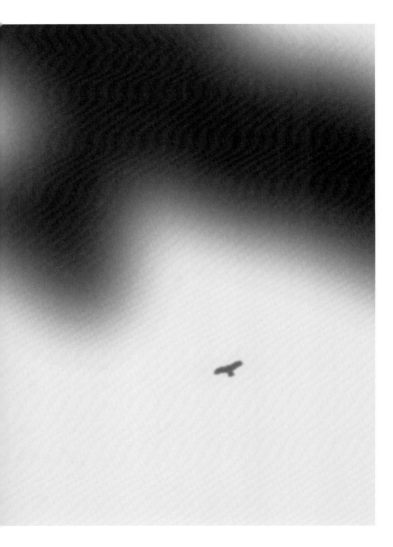

AIR | Depth: Expression through Shadows

PAIR

When the A.D. era began, there were about 100 million people. There are seventy times as many today. The population has increased in a geometric progression, and mankind looks like it's headed for large-scale extinction. Considering the survival of three generations hence, we can neither deny ourselves the treats before our eyes nor refrain from having children. I wonder if this is the extent of man's intelligence.

Society has implicitly encouraged "pairing," taking effect as unwritten social rules, taboos, systems, and wisdom, with the aim of controlling our instincts.

On the other hand, today there's less pressure to pair up; we've entered a new era in human relationships. Independent individuals connect via networks. I wonder if the relationship between two people is, after all, the method by which one individual and the other clash with one another while groping, together, for optimum comfort. Is the premise for the diversity necessary for transmitting superior genes losing its meaning because of the fading significance of propagation? Either way, for students, this question holds no authenticity. Unmaterialized "Love" still occupies the center of their existence. They are simply life, not yet thinking reeds.

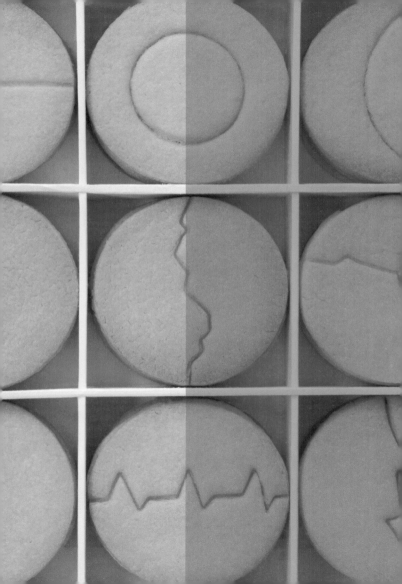

1 You

Keisuke TSUBAKIMOTO

This photographic series was an attempt to depict a twosome by capturing one person in the eye of another. As a photographic technique, it is not at all easy to take a picture of a person not looking through one's own eye, but reflected in the eye of another.

Keisuke Tsubakimoto devised this close-up technique and applied it diligently to get a number of photos.

Consequently, his work has evolved into a series of unique portraits mediated by the eye of specific individuals, rather than mere photographs of an eye reflecting the figure of a person. It is also interesting to make us feel that the sensory organs we call *eyes* are tinged with a strange solemnity. The cornea is covered with a thin film of water, and in the reflection on the cornea, transformed into a wet mirror surface, appears the subject at which the eye is staring. Indeed, we fall into a mysterious illusion, as if the image of life were captured by that water-covered planet, Earth. The series also shows us a macroscopic perspective in which before we are individuals, we are part of an immense circle of life.

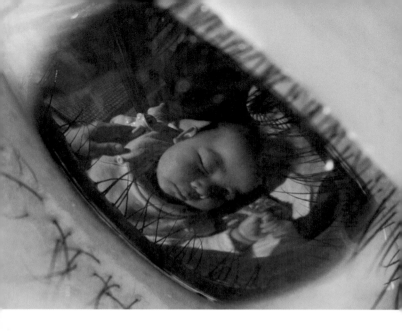

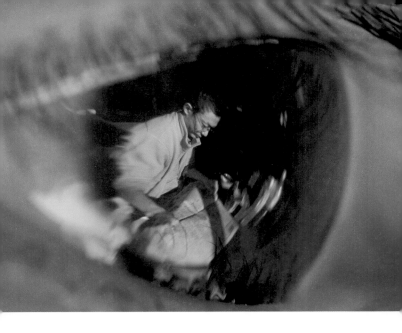

PAIR | You

PAIR | You

2   Mutual Soap

Harumi SASAKI

Everyone has probably attached the last tiny nub of a used bar of soap to a new one. We're hardly going to throw away the little bit that remains to finish it up, we stick it to a new bar to make it the perfect size to use. Harumi Sasaki focused on this aspect of soap. In these forms of mingled soaps, she may have discovered for us humanity's mutual and earnest mindfulness, as well as a subtle sense of humor.

The lumpy pieces of soap have a piquancy, and can be seen as beautiful. The very feeling of cherishing these features might lead a person to new awareness and understanding of design. I guess Sasaki intends to use these phenomena as a design for soap. Within her intention to design for produced soap, there's a sharp insight into human psychology: we have an awareness of others. This work is delicate yet stately. Within her focus can be sensed firm conviction.

PAIR | Mutual Soap

Choose one from a great number of combinations.
Make a mold of it and reproduce it as a product.
See the image of the mass produced product
(next page).

mutual soap

A figure of a pair of soap melting together.

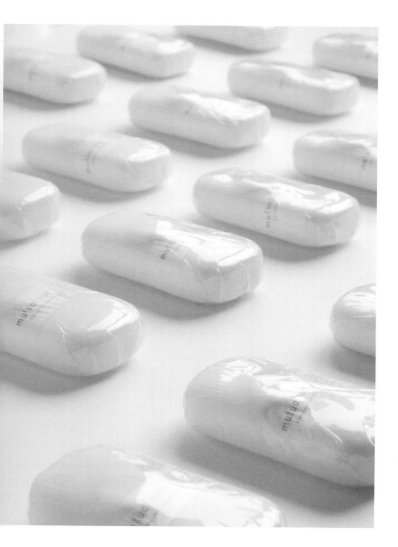

PAIR | Mutual Soap

3 X-ray Portraits

Saiko KANDA

Mayuka HAYASHI

Saiko Kanda and Mayuka Hayashi tried making photographic portraits with X-rays. They reflect physical similarities and differences between humans in terms of the layers of bone structures. We can also detect excellent focus in their portraits of twosomes. There are already many examples of X-ray radiography art, and work using the X-rays of a kiss. However, their work is superb in its careful calculation of the photographs, taken in order to capture directly symbolic twosome portraits, with the premise being visual representation of the penetration of flesh leaving only bones. Maybe this is a meticulously planned photographic exposure of individual differences. We deeply sense their originality as portraits; the overlapping of the twins' transparent bodies discloses the notable proximity of twins, thereby unveiling their individual differences. The elaborate production process deserves our recognition. It was performed within photographic opportunities that were extremely constrained by restrictions on radiation doses. And the images are beautiful, allowing for artistic fixing that very subtly evokes lyricism while transcending the level of technology-oriented fixing commonly found in this kind of work.

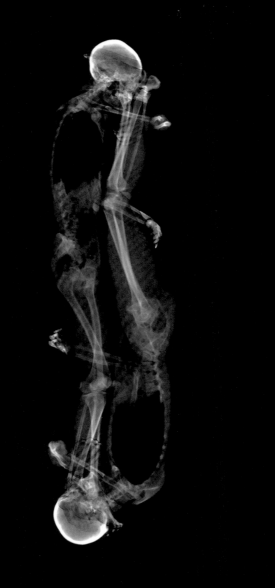

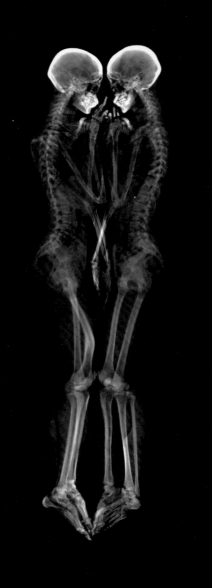

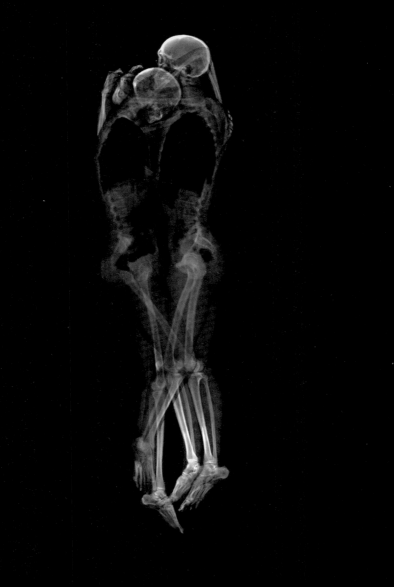

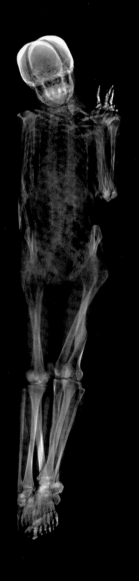

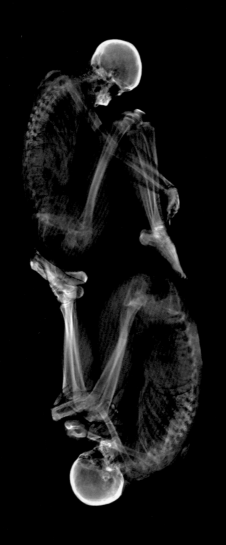

4   Courts

Hiroko AOKI

What if a tennis court were twice the usual size? Surely the larger part would be settled by the serve. The current sizes of the court and service box are limited by the field in which the return might land. That is, the court as a spatial condition is the premise for all of the athletes' activities. The sumo arena is the same. If the sumo arena were two-thirds the size, or square, the circumstances of the competition would certainly change quite a bit.

Hiroko Aoki focused on the court as rules like this that restrict the relationship between pairs of athletes. In sports competitions, the court is a symbol of rules on which pairs (of athletes) are imposed. The established rules are the premise by which training is conducted, equipment evolves, and strategy is determined. The traces of the ball and the footsteps of the wrestlers are vestiges of acts guided by the existing authoritative rules. Reviewing the court from these viewpoints produces something fresh and beautiful.

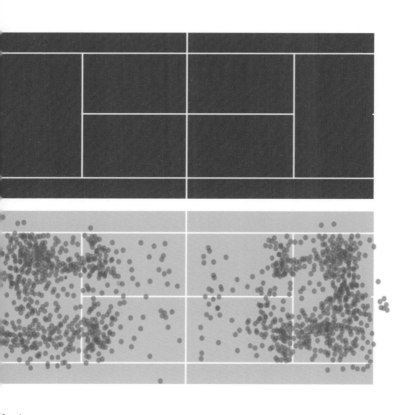

Tennis

These are the points of contact between ball and court in
the final match of the Wimbledon Championships in 2010.
R. Nadal vs N. Djokovic

PAIR | Courts

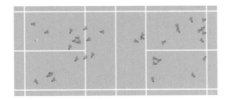

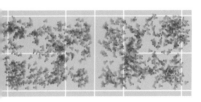

Badminton
All-Japan Comprehensive Badminton
Championships
Shuttlecock landing points, 2011 final
Sho Sasaki vs Kenichi Tago

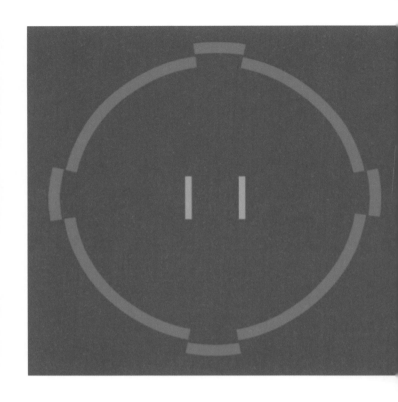

Sumo
2012 Autumn Grand Sumo Tournament
Wrestlers' footprints
Harumafuji vs Hakuho

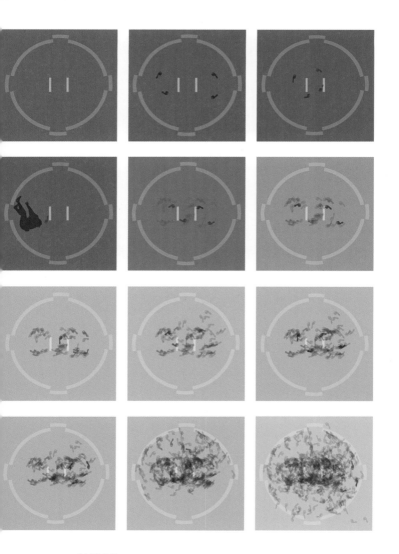

5   Halfsies

Kyoko OSAKI

When two people split something, emotions are complicated. When two people fall in love with the same person, it's hard to find a solution that pleases both of them. However, there are quite a few things on which we can go halfsies. For instance, cookies. What kinds of methods are there to break a single cookie by hand for two people to share? They could draw straws, and the winner could break the cookie in two and choose which part he or she wants. Or they could crush it more finely, and take turns choosing the biggest portion until all the pieces are gone. This way, there might be a little more equality than in the first case. Or, thinking a little more humbly, one could break it in two and give the larger piece to the other.

In any case, this research reflects the subtlety of the psychology of dividing and dispensing directly onto cookie design. It makes a strong point to the degree that I want to make this into a product exactly as it is. It's also interesting that even if someone eats the cookie alone, he's going to feel as if two selves are sprouting within.

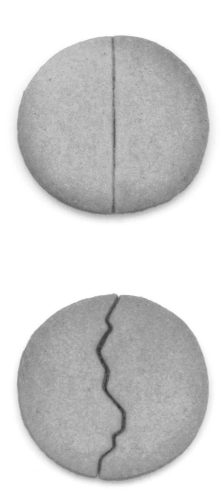

PAIR | Halfsies

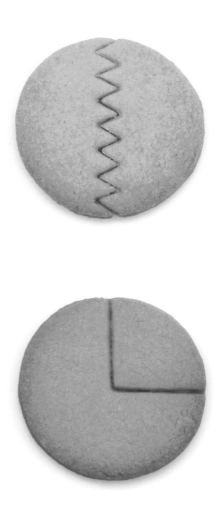

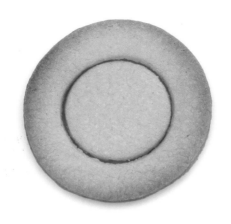

PAIR | Halfsies

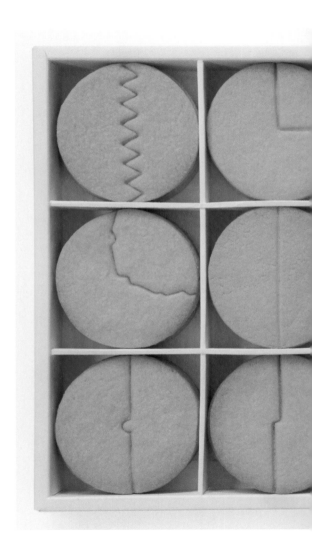

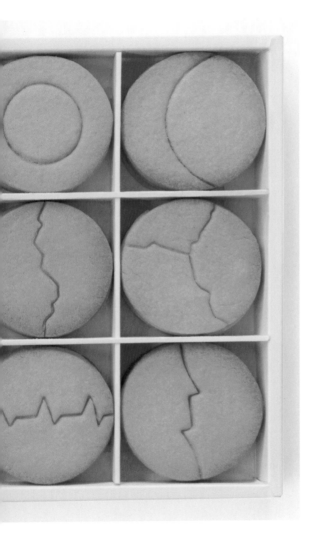

PAIR | Halfsies

6 Between

Shoko SAKUTA

Edward Hall perceived the distance between people as a code symbolizing human relationships. He authored "The Hidden Dimension." Shoko Sakuta expresses this invisible thing with kokeshi* she made herself. Their facial expressions and relationship seem to change depending on subtle differences in the distance between them and their facial orientation. It may seem simple, but implementation was difficult and took a long time, because, to convey every human relationship, the kokeshi's facial expression has to be free from gender and age. It must be like, or rather over and above, a Noh mask,** as its face should embody the ultimately expressionless face, reflecting delicate situations or feelings. Sakuta had the necessary technique, and manipulated the photographic environment in such a way that she was able to capture magnificently the kokeshis' pure relationship. There is no wavering in intention or method; this is excellent research.

*Kokeshi: Traditional Japanese wooden doll turned on a lathe whose simple form is comprised of a spherical head and cylindrical body.
**Noh mask: Mask worn by actors in Noh plays. The ko-omote mask has the richest variety of facial expressions, communicating joy, anger, pathos and humor.

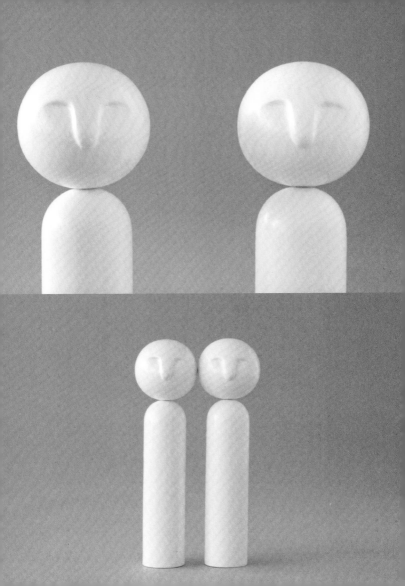

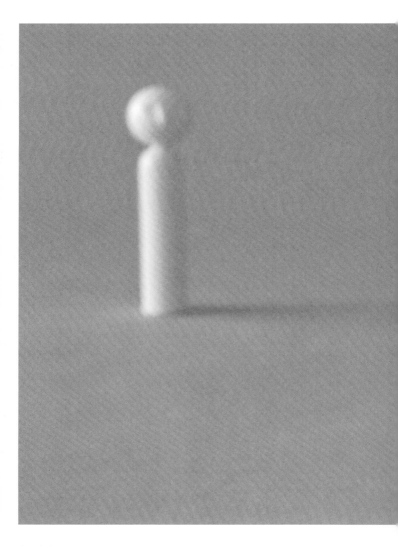

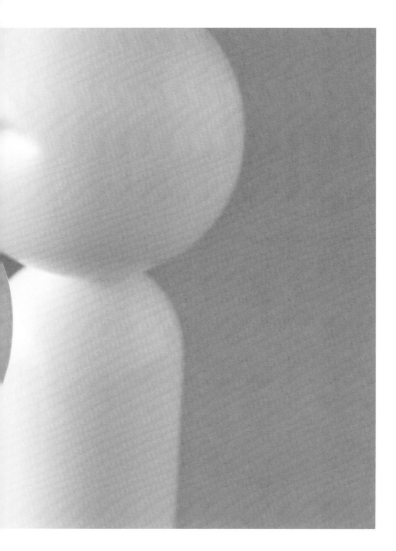

PAIR | Between

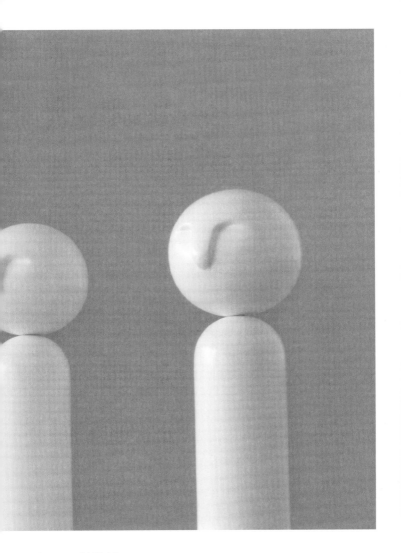

PAIR | Between

7   Boxed Lunches

Eri NAKAGAWA

In Japan, we call boxed lunches O-bento. The bento is part of our food culture, arising from the staple, rice, which can be tightly packed into a container. We are good at cramming into the bento not only rice, but also the main dish of meat or fish, vegetables, and side dishes of pickles and such. Even today, many use the bento as a way to ensure nutritional balance and save money. Eri Nakagawa focused on the packing of the bento, reading pair as symmetrical. Tamagoyaki, or a rolled egg omelet, is arranged symmetrically, but achieving symmetry all the way down to the grains of rice is difficult. However, if handled patiently, green peas and black sesame seeds can be made symmetrical. As a fillet, salmon keeps its symmetry hidden within. The minimalistic array of rolled sushi impresses anew. The ultimate piece is the bento in which two umeboshi, or pickled plums, are arranged symmetrically: the ideal "bento for two."

PAIR | Boxed Lunches

PAIR | Boxed Lunches

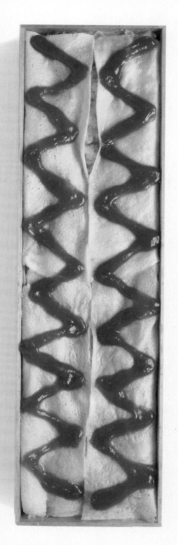

PAIR | Boxed Lunches

TOKYO

The 10th Ex-formation theme was Tokyo/Seoul, and was carried out at two universities, one in each city. With participation by Kim Kyung-kyun at Korea National University of Arts, who showed interest in Ex-formation, students from each university focused on the city in which their own campus is located. Because the basic theme was "one's own city" we'll cover Tokyo here. We cannot be objective about the city in which we live. We've never seen a guidebook of our own city. Tokyo has a very well-developed railway system, but we didn't start using it after studying it; we became familiar with it gradually, through use. There are vending machines and convenience stores everywhere. It's a megacity with a population of 13 million, but for us, it's our normal environment. We're familiar with Tokyo, and so to just that extent, we've stopped being able to see it. It's just like how people who are healthy don't recognize the reality of health. A small awakening has occurred every time I've returned from traveling abroad. This is an appropriate theme to punctuate the long journey known as Ex-formation.

1 Tokyo Komon: The City's New Traditional Pattern

Moeno SUZUKI

Edo komon are textile patterns with subjects derived from the everyday environment and used for kimono during the isolationist period known as the Edo era. They are not simply geometrical repetitions of figures; the point was to demonstrate an acuity of perception of everyday scenery and customs to turn into patterns, with casual buoyancy and quirkiness. People wore komon-patterned kimono eagerly and competitively. The look was casual but fashion-conscious, and patterns grew in sophistication. The komon plays a part in Japan's traditional textiles. Tokyo Komon grew from Moeno Suzuki's motif choices and good sense. She perfected patterns that reverberate with the Edo era's refined insight and are based on the daily scenery and customs of today's Tokyo. This research notes the associations of sensibility, the cultural genes inherited by Tokyo from Edo. The "traditions" of the Tokyo youth community today are also portrayed in patterns ensconced within Suzuki's style: chain link fences, Tokyo Tower, the electromagnetic wave icon and the tactile paving tiles dotting the city's streets and sidewalks. Consequently, they are perfectly suited to beautifully grace the wrapping cloths known as *furoshiki*.

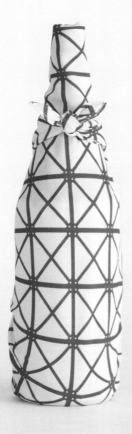

TOKYO | Tokyo Komon: The City's New Traditional Pattern

Left: Tokyo Komon, by Moeno Suzuki
Right: Traditional Edo komon

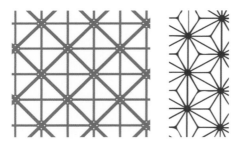

Tokyo Tower Komon (left)
and Edo komon Hemp leaves

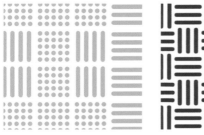

Tactile paving komon (left)
and Edo komon Sankuzushi
[three-line cobblestone pattern]

Wi-Fi (left)
and Edo komon Wave crest pattern

Raven komon (left)
and Edo komon Plovers

Fence komon (left)
and Edo komon Hinoki
(J. cypress) fence

TOKYO | Tokyo Komon: The City's New Traditional Pattern

2   Tokyo Masks

Sachi KODERA

Sachi Kodera morphed the facial images of a hundred men and a hundred women to create an average male face and an average female face. The technique known as morphing is a strange thing; as the number of samples grew, individual idiosyncrasies, even glasses and hairstyles, were absorbed into the averaging process and faded away. However, within that averaging, the personality of Japan, or rather, of the city of Tokyo, firmly materialized. The glasses and trendy hairstyles we'd expect to disappear completely in blending remained definite influences, and Tokyo's individuality was actualized as two faces.

Kodera created three-dimensional masks out of the finished images, and photographed various people wearing them. The average faces, with their symmetry and uniformity, make a beautiful woman and a handsome man. Or rather, perhaps the average face, with few variations, is what is called "a beautiful woman" or "a handsome man." Accordingly, these are the faces of Tokyo's beautiful women and handsome men. Photographs of the average good-looking face applied to passersby gives one a strange sense of incongruity. This feeling itself may be Tokyo's reality.

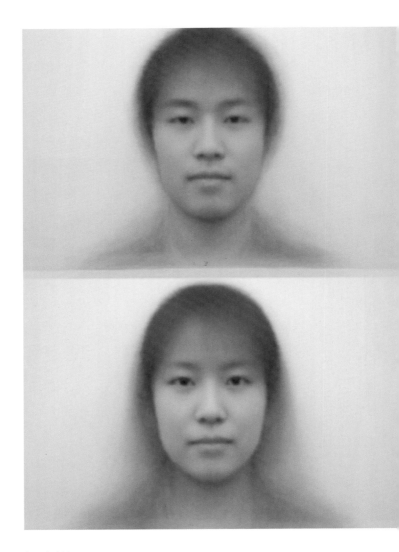

Production of the mask of averages:
Collect the facial images of a hundred men and
a hundred women in Tokyo,
use morphing software to create one average face
for each gender. (left-hand page)
Above is the printout of the plaster mask based on this data.

We had people put on the masks in various locations
around Tokyo and took their pictures.

Asakusa (left)
Harajuku (right)

3   Tokyo Cup Noodles

Yurika SUZUKI

Yurika Suzuki, with a good analytic eye, accurately captures the features and details of each highly individual neighborhood fashion, whether that of the youth of Shibuhara* or the business suits common to Shinbashi. Suzuki's intuition led her to liken Tokyo to cup noodles.** Her creations are divided into distinct locales: Ginza, Akihabara, Shinbashi, Asakusa, and Tokyo; the individually dressed citizens are expressed as ingredients. Presumably, the noodles are the city's air, which connects the people, and the soup, the ambience.

Instant cup noodles are not traditional Japanese food. Today they're commonly eaten with disposable chopsticks, but at first they were eaten with a small plastic fork. Modern rationality has mingled with Japanese pop culture, producing Japanese fast food. To be told that Tokyo resembles this gives one mixed feelings, but it can't be denied.

*Shibuhara: A coined term that blends two Tokyo neighborhoods where young people hang out: Shibuya and Harajuku.
**Cup noodles: An instant noodle product developed in Japan in the 1970s. The consumer tears off the paper lid, adds boiling water into the disposable cup, and waits three minutes before eating.

SHIMBASHI Cup Noodle
Shimbashi, packed with middle-aged "salarymen"...
Japan's busy salarymen seem somewhat tired.

GINZA Cup Noodle
Rich middle-aged women,
carrying top-brand purses and shopping bags,
walking along the streets of Ginza.

AKIHABARA Cup Noodle
Akihabara: Nerds, waitresses in "maid cafés," consumer electronics-packed streets… Nerds wearing t-shirts bearing images of their favorite anime characters.

ASAKUSA Cup Noodle
Foreign tourists, junior high schoolers on trips
from the countryside… Rickshaws, sumo wrestlers.
Asakusa has all the classic tourist attractions.

4   Tokyo Camouflage

Haruka MATSUBARA

You laugh in spite of yourself when you see photos or videos of this camouflage clothing, and you may even miss the people wearing them, if you're not paying attention. That's how well they blend in. Combat camouflage frightens us, but the singularity of this research lies in applying the concept to a peaceful city. It's fun and challenging to blend into a bustling downtown street, but we don't normally think of camouflaging ourselves in residential neighborhoods. Matsubara calmly indexed elements of the urban landscape—characters written on the surfaces of streets and alleys, insipid cinderblock walls, blue signs indicating domicile addresses—and audaciously arranged them on clothing, admirably creating camo clothing for various neighborhoods of Tokyo. The selected neighborhoods, like Asakusa and Marunouchi, have scenic features with which we're already likely acquainted, but this project makes us encounter their distinctive features from an odd angle. The moment the viewer apprehends the effect of the camouflage, clueing him or her into the particulars of the neighborhood, the laugh and the understanding come simultaneously; the unknowing of the subject and the deepening of understanding proceed apace.

SHINJUKU

SETAGAYA

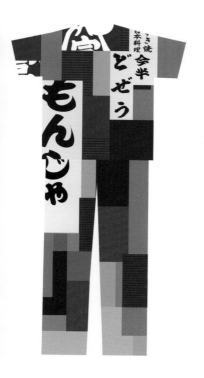

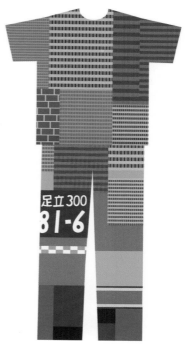

ASAKUSA

MARUNOUCHI

TOKYO | Tokyo Camouflage

Verified by video recording…
We videotaped the wearing of camo
in each neighborhood.
We couldn't even see the models
until they'd drawn near.

5   Tokyo Okaki

Natsumi MATSUMOTO

The phrase *kaki no tane** in addition to indicating the seed(*tane*) of the persimmon(*kaki*), also indicates a very popular snack in Japan, which features thin asymmetrical roasted rice crackers. Tiny, crispy, and crunchy, kaki no tane became popular in a mix with just the right proportion of peanuts, and has fully penetrated daily life in Japan. Among the snacks known as *o-tsumami*** this one plays a leading role. A bag brimming with kaki no tane is like rice, easy to pick up with one's fingers and easy to eat. It's no exaggeration to say that it's become one of Japan's signature features! First of all, it's an interesting concept to relate people to kaki no tane. The excellence of Natsumi Matsumoto's analogy is in the overlap between the image of crackers, each one different from the next, crammed into a bag, and the crowding of people into the largest metropolis in the world. We can nod in agreement with the variety of metaphors Matsumoto devised for these snacks, whether arranged in a line or a circle, packed tightly into a bag, coupled with peanuts or alone.

*Kaki no tane: A snack made of glutinous rice shaped like the seed of a persimmon, brushed with soy sauce, and baked.
**Snacks like this that are picked up with the fingertips (verb: tsumamu) are called o-tsumami.

TOKYO | Tokyo Okaki

TOKYO | Tokyo Okaki

Traditionally prizing the spirit of mass cooperation,
Japanese tend toward the forming of queues.
When the crackers line up, they look like a queue.

The smallest unit of this snack is "human."
This time, they are placed holding hands in a circle.
They can also be seen as Japanese who love acts of
conformity.

Singles, couples, nuclear families…
This is how the creator herself saw it.
Or are the nuts partners of the opposite sex?

6   Tokyo Pulsation

Xin ZHONG

What if you tried to distill the true movement of Tokyo's trains? It's been done in this project, a splendid visualization achieved through diligent data notation. Xin Zhong took the timetables for the commuting hours, weekday mornings between 8:00 and 8:59 and 9:00 and 9:59, when the most railway cars are in operation, indexed the number and movement of trains, and presented it as a video. The video conveys a pulsating aspect of the railway network that supports Tokyo's powerful transportation infrastructure, including the Chuo and Yamanote train lines and the Ginza subway line. The unusual complexity and precision of Tokyo's railway movement is not found in Seoul, London, Beijing, Jakarta, or New York. This very movement creates an impression of Tokyo's great vitality. Shinjuku Station, serving more than 700,000 passengers per day, is apparently the world's busiest, but this is not because of the scale of Shinjuku or of its station. It is because of the dynamism and the volume created by the fluidity and mobility of the entire intricately linked rail network. The images Xin Zhong produced are small and delicate, but they have precisely captured the dynamism of this megacity.

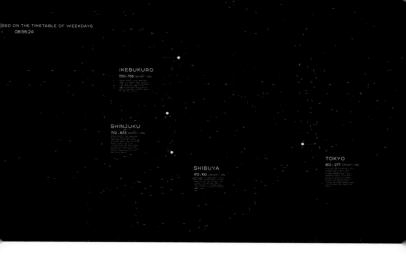

BASED ON THE TIMETABLE OF WEEKDAYS
08:56:24

IKEBUKURO
550,756 people / day

SHINJUKU
749,833 people / day

SHIBUYA
412,100 people / day

TOKYO
402,277 people / day

TOKYO PULSATION

Tokyo, as the centre of the Greater Tokyo Area, is Japan's largest domestic and international hub for rail, ground, and air transportation. Public transportation within Tokyo is dominated by an extensive network of clean and efficient trains and subways run by a variety of operators, with buses, monorails and trams playing a secondary feeder role.

Scan the QR code,
watch the video.

TOKYO | Tokyo Pulsation

Afterword and Looking Forward to a New Ex-formation

Kenya HARA

Published in this book are the products of the development of my seminars undertaken in the Department of The Science of Design at Tokyo's Musashino Art University, research results photographed and recorded by the students themselves. For ten years beginning in 2004, the results of Ex-formation have been published in Japan, one volume per year. I am proud of the fact that we have been able to publish every single product of every single student, without a single dropout. Now, summarizing the work of a decade, I regret having to pick and choose, but this is probably necessary in order to dispatch our results in a way that's easy to understand in an international context. In honor of the research of all of my seminar students, I noted all of their names and the titles of their work in the appendix.

In the middle of my project, I found out that the term *exformation* was used in *The User Illusion*, a book by the Danish science journalist Tor Norretranders. However, he uses *exformation* to indicate outside information, or extra information which, if excised, does not impair the purpose of the message. Recognizing that Norretranders's "exformation" is used as a completely different term, I've decided to continue to use the term *Ex-formation*, having clearly defined its meaning.

This decade of research into Ex-formation was a fresh experiment in communication design, not only for my students, but also for me. I want to note that the research published here was our first implementation, in every sense of the word. To be able to conduct research with these fledgling sensibilities is the reason I keep coming to the university. We designers are not information consumers. We are information masters. The goal of information design is not to define something, nor to make it understood. It is to motivate people's curiosity and elicit action. The era in which design is simply a function is fast coming to an end. Design is the wisdom that will rejuvenate the world, visualizing dormant possibilities and offering people a fresh awakening. It is not describing things nor interpreting them. It is arousing the possibility for things to become unknown. I want to entrust the world to youth who are armed with such inspiring wisdom as they leave the nest.

I used to tell my students, "Think with the mind-set of others." This doesn't mean to have someone else come up with ideas for you. It means that if you move things forward based on how you feel, your products will be equally pretentious. Because design is a practice predicated on universality, it's important to ask oneself not "How do I feel?" but rather "How does everyone feel?" The themes covered by Ex-formation are broad, but because students proceeded with their own research while letting their feelings and thoughts reverberate among themselves, I believe that the examples published here can be shared by all people. I hope, from the bottom of my heart, that through the publication of this volume, even more awakenings will come about.

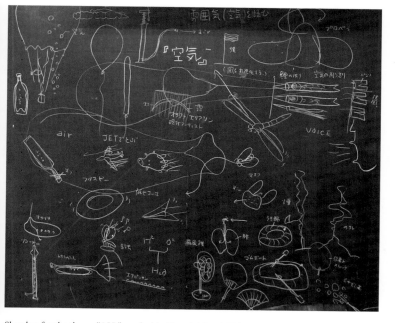

Sketches for the theme "AIR" on the blackboad. May, 2014

Appendix

Due to space limitations, we were not able to include the work of all of the students of the past ten years. I am extremely happy to have had the opportunity to conduct this decade of Ex-formation research without a single student dropping out of the program. Here, I would like to thank all the students once again, and at the same time share the results of our work.

RIVER (Shimanto River)

2004

"Simulations:
If the River were a Road"
Shinsaku Inaba,
Sousuke Matsushita
and Hirofumi Mori

"Footprint Landscape: Stepping
on the Shimanto River"
Kyoko Nakamura,
Kazuko Nomoto
and Kaori Hashimoto

"Collecting"
Akari Ono, Asako Tadano

"Hexahedron: The Shimanto
River Cut into Cubes"
Aiko Yoshihara

"Scenes of Time"
Kazuko Nomoto, Aiko Yoshihara

"Poly-sight"
Kazuko Nomoto

"So Many People, So Many Rivers"
Mika Ikeda, Tamaki Oyama,
Maiko Kato and Taiko Kanemichi

"Catch and Eat 6
Six Days Alone: The Document"
Kouichirou Uno

published by Chuokoron-Shinsha, Inc., Tokyo

RESORT

2005

"Vinyl / Stripes"
Emiko Ai

"Sleeping Outside"
Makiko Orihara, Yukari Kimura,
Satoko Takahasi and Hiroko Mori

"Soft Creamer"
Shino Ito, Aya Kazama
and Mona Tanaka

"Loose Typography"
Kazu Yanagisawa

"Daily Resort"
Tomoko Shinozuka

"Resort Switch"
Makoto Tomita

"Hiragana Phonetic Characters"
Asuka Ishii

"Moments of Tea"
Hiroko Nagai

"Atamihon:
Atami…Condensed Japan"
Yuki Sumikawa, Takashi Honda
and Syu Watanabe

published by Chuokoron-Shinsha, Inc., Tokyo

WRINKLES

2006

"Egg: A Collection of Wrinkles"
Yukimi Kushige

"Sent Wrinkles"
Emi Tsukada, Yutaka Hirose
and Yukina Matsumoto

"Wrinkled Products"
Koutarou Fujita, Kazuya Morita
and Yojiro Watanabe

"Complex Trail:
The Rivers and Roads of Japan"
Chie Uchida, Aki Takada

"Wrinkle Factory"
Natsuno Kanoh

"Pillows"
Yuko Sato

"Cast Islands"
Tomoko Nishi

"Wrinkle Patterns"
Mina Ko, Aya Hayase

"Aging"
Eriko Sigihara

"Words as Wrinkles:
Collecting Traces of Emotion"
Yoko Kageyama

"A Study of Wrinkles"
Yoshinori Ishikawa

published by Chuokoron-Shinsha, Inc., Tokyo

PLANTS

2007

published by Heibonsha, Inc., Tokyo

NUDITY

2008

"Materials and Nudity"
Kent Iitaka, Junya Maejima

"Nude Dolls"
Kaede Endo

"Nude Comics for Girls"
Istumi Yokokura, Keiko Yokoyama

"Undies Project"
Sachie Murakami

"Undressing Completion"
Eriko Takayanagi

"Naked Nude"
Nao Akiya

"Nude Color"
Ai Tooyama

"Buttocks"
Kota Fujikawa, Aya Funaki

"Revelation through Eating"
Yuhei Funabiki

"The Naked Earth"
Tsubura Kobayashi

"Undressing Information"
Masahiro Watahiki

published by Heibonsha, Inc., Tokyo

WOMAN

2009

"People who Give Birth"
Yuka Okazaki

"Lovely Ware"
Megumi Kawagoe, Yu Kawana
and Eriko Fujii

"Flora"
Asuka Tada

"Stick Figures"
Anri Yamada

"Nice Body PET Bottles"
Keisuke Nakano

"Secret Flower Garden"
Koki Takeya

"Woman's Poker Face"
Kiyoe Kobayashi

"Doll House"
Shohei Sawada

"A Girl and A Woman"
Yuko Sasaki

"Behaving like A Graceful Woman"
Chika Goto

"Expecting"
Riho Kurihara

"Looking at the Woman
Looked at by a Woman"
Ken Nakazawa

"Decipher Women through
Playing Cards Together"
Nana Yoshiura

published by Heibonsha, Inc., Tokyo

HALF-DONE

2010

"Ladybirds"
Eriko Akata

"Before Baked"
Midori Yamamoto, Sari Yukawa

"Stuffed Toys"
Katsuya Yamamoto

"Cast-off Skin / Second Birth"
Natsumi Toyoda

"Obscure"
Megumi Nishina

"Hazy Memories"
Nozomi Nishiyama

"The Pathos of Things"
Chie Tsunekawa

"Peach Fuzz"
Madoka Takemura

"Twilight Specs"
Yu Iijima

"Incomplete"
Hiroki Fujimaki

"Room for Improvement"
Mizuki Iwane

published by Heibonsha, Inc., Tokyo

AIR

2011

"Undulations"
Aoi Moriya

"Wearing the Bulge"
Akane Onuki

"Holes"
Seiji Tahara

"Framing the Air"
Dahye Song

"If the Air Were Made of
Orange Particles"
Shiori Kamo

"Windows:
Looking through the Air"
Maki Ota

"Imaginable"
Heejin Lee

"The Circumstances of Moss"
Shota Kimura

"Depth:
Expression through Shadows"
Kinuko Ohshima, Chie Sakakura
and Shogo Mori

"Flutter"
Saki Igarashi, Yoko Nakano

"Body"
Kota Suda

"Wings and Spinning"
Sumireko Shibukawa

"Airy: Weaving the Air"
Mana Yamamoto

published by Heibonsha, Inc., Tokyo

EX-FORMATION

Author	Kenya Hara
Editorial concept	Kenya Hara, Lars Müller
Translation	Maggie Kinser Hohle, Yukiko Naito
Book design	Kenya Hara + Tomoko Nishi
	Hara Design Institute, Nippon Design Center, Inc.
Copyediting	Keonaona Peterson
Proofreading	Sarah Quigley
Publishing	Lars Müller Publishers
	Zurich, Switzerland
	www.lars-mueller-publishers.com
Printing and Binding	Belvédère Art Books, Oosterbeek, the Netherlands

Distributed in the North America by ARTBOOK | D.A.P.
www.artbook.com

ISBN 978-3-03778-466-2

Printed in the Netherlands

Kenya HARA

Designer Kenya Hara (b. 1958) emphasizes the design of both objects and experiences.

In 2000, he produced the exhibition "RE-DESIGN—Daily Products of the 21st Century," which successfully presented the fact that the resources of astonishing design are found in the context of the very ordinary and casual. In 2002, Hara became a member of MUJI's advisory board and began acting as its art director. In 2004, he planned and directed the exhibition "HAPTIC—Awakening the Senses" revealing to the audience that great resources of design are dormant in the human senses. Much of his work, including the programs for the Opening and Closing Ceremonies of the Nagano Winter Olympic Games and Expo 2005, is deeply rooted in Japanese culture. In 2007 and 2009, he produced two exhibitions titled "TOKYO FIBER—SENSEWARE" in Paris, Milan, and Tokyo, and from 2008 through 2009, the exhibition "JAPAN CAR" in Paris and at the Science Museum in London. Hara's focus in these kinds of exhibitions is on visualizing and widely disseminating the potentiality of industry. The radius of his activity has been expanding to the rest of Asia as well, including the traveling exhibition "DESIGNING DESIGN—Kenya Hara 2011 China Exhibition" that started in Beijing in 2011. Several books authored by Hara, including *Designing Design* and *White*, have been translated into a number of languages, including other Asian languages.

President, the Nippon Design Center Inc.
Professor at Musashino Art University
President, Japan Design Committee Co., Ltd.
Vice President, Japan Graphic Designers Association Inc.

SEOUL / TOKYO

2013

"Tokyo Dome This,
Tokyo Dome That"
Kayo Ikeda

"Town without Letters"
Hikari Imamura

"Tokyo Mask"
Sachi Kodera

"Tokyo in One Stroke"
Ryoko Shiono

"Tokyo Pulsation"
Xin Zhong

"Tokyo Komon: The City's
New Traditional Patterns"
Moeno Suzuki

"Tokyo Cup Noodles"
Yurika Suzuki

"Tokyo Buildings"
Saki Toya

"Tokyo Camouflage"
Haruka Matsubara

"Tokyo Okaki"
Natsumi Matsumoto

"Sushi Pillow"
Tomotaka Miyagawa

"Tokyo Crows"
Mizuho Yamaguchi

published by Doosung Books Co., Ltd. Seoul

PAIR

2012

"You"
Keisuke Tsubakimoto

"Mutual Soap"
Harumi Sasaki

"X-ray Portraits"
Saiko Kanda, Mayuka Hayashi

"Courts"
Hiroko Aoki

"Halfsies"
Kyoko Osaki

"One"
Yuri Iio

"Between"
Shoko Sakuta

"Strange Pair"
Kotono Oda

"Proxemics: A Bench for You and Me"
Risa Takahashi

"Women in The Tale of Genji"
Riko Koide

"Male / Female"
Asuka Suzuki

"Cacti Relations"
Tomoka Sugamata

"Two Pairs"
Ami Tamura

"Lunch Box"
Eri Nakagawa

published by Heibonsha, Inc., Tokyo